THE ART OF WEAVING

THE ART OF WEAVING

ELSE REGENSTEINER

VAN NOSTRAND REINHOLD COMPANY

NEW YORK   CINCINNATI   TORONTO   LONDON   MELBOURNE

Frontispiece:
Detail of Fig. 8-4, "The World Is Shimmering,"
tapestry by Josefina Robirosa.

Van Nostrand Reinhold Company Regional Offices:
New York Cincinnati Chicago Millbrae Dallas

Van Nostrand Reinhold Company International Offices:
London Toronto Melbourne

Copyright © 1970 by Litton Educational Publishing, Inc.

Library of Congress Catalog Card Number 76-110062

ISBN 0 442 22672 6 (paper)
ISBN 0 442 11442 7 (cloth)

Designed by Myron Hall III
Line drawings by George McVicker
Photographs by Edward Miller except where otherwise credited
Drafts by Takeko Nomiya

Published by Van Nostrand Reinhold Company
135 West 50th Street, New York, N.Y. 10020

16 15 14 13 12 11 10 9

No book on weaving can pretend to be the complete
invention of its author. It can only be built upon the
wealth of experiences of many weavers who have
shared their knowledge in books, articles and studios.
I am deeply grateful to the authors of the books included in the bibliography and to the many artists who
contributed their creative work for the illustrations.

I wish to express special thanks to Edward Miller,
who uncomplainingly photographed hundreds of textiles; to George McVicker, who did the drawings; to
Takeko Nomiya, who made the drafts; and to Janet
Kravetz, who typed the manuscript.

Sincere thanks for their generous permission to use
specific drafts and directions are extended to Eunice
Anders, Peter Collingwood, Meda Johnston, Madeleine
Smith, Mary Alice Smith, Lurene Stone, John Kennardh
White, and to the late Harriet Tidball.

I gratefully acknowledge the help and encouragement given me by Dean Roger Gilmore of the School
of the Art Institute of Chicago and by my son-in-law,
Herman Sinaiko, who constructively discussed with
me the intricacies of the English language. No words
can express my gratitude to Nancy C. Newman who,
while weaving only with her mind, edited the manuscript with skill and understanding. And last but not
least, I thank my husband for his unfailing patience and
equanimity, with which he helped me over many rough
spots during the writing of the book.

I am happy and proud that the following artists whose
work is included in this book are present or former
students of mine at the School of the Art Institute of
Chicago: Terry Albright, Ruta Bremanis, Shelley Chris-
tensen, Diane Craig, Nancy Crump, Barbara Fine, Ben-
jamin Gladfelter, Jay Hinz, Linda Howard, Helena
Jacobson, Lloyd Johnson, Delma Kelly, Darlyne Kasper,
Roanne Katz, Joanna Kiljanska, Sharon Kouris, Lois
Lebov, Gwynne Lott, Cynthia Lubliner, Barbara Meyer,
Takeko Nomiya, Natalie Novotny, Dorothy Novotny,
Michi Ouchi, Joel W. Plum, Jane Redman, Rickie von
Reitzenstein, Marci Riedel, Jon Riis, Richard Scrozyn-
ski, Llubica Stevanov, Leora K. Stewart, Jennifer Stewart,
Astra Strobel, Molly Simons, Diane Wiersba, Diane
White, John Kennardh White, Jean Young, Sue Zinn-
grabe, Marsha Ford Anderle, Napoleon Henderson,
Oliver Wittasek, Carolyn Saberniak.

CONTENTS

INTRODUCTION

"Weaving was never like this before!" exclaimed an art critic at a display of contemporary woven wall hangings. His words illustrate vividly the enormous versatility of the age-old craft, emerging fresh and new in modern form.

The tentative twisting of fiber into thread and the first interlocking of yarn to form fabric were the beginning of one of the most significant landmarks in man's history. The student who has never given textiles a thought is in the position of primitive man, about to discover the thrill of a new creative medium, with the addition of the sophisticated developments of modern technology.

Weaving has many faces: it is a craft, a medium for working directly with fundamental materials to create joyful mixtures of textures and colors, to feel the accomplishment of mastering the tools and learning the steps, and to explore the discipline of fine craftsmanship. It is an art, an expression of our time, which can have the brilliance of a painting, the dimension of sculpture, the shape of invention, and the form of imagination. It is functional, intimately related to us through our daily use of fabrics. It is an industrial product made speedily by the power loom, but unchanged in its basic construction of interlocking threads, and it is as individual as its creator will make it. It is a tool for the educator and a technique for the therapist; it is romantic and sober, ancient and contemporary.

As with all crafts, fundamentals and theory must be learned before the full range of creative possibilities can be embraced. But invention can start together with learning, and technical perfection does not have to be dull. This book is a guide, intended to open doors to as many faces of weaving as knowledge, imagination, and inspiration can conceive.

"Head," tapestry weave by Esther Gotthoffer. (Photo: Lodder)

"Faces," laid-in weaves by Jane Redman.

"Face," tapestry in wool yarns by Jane Redman.
Slit, soumak, and rya techniques.

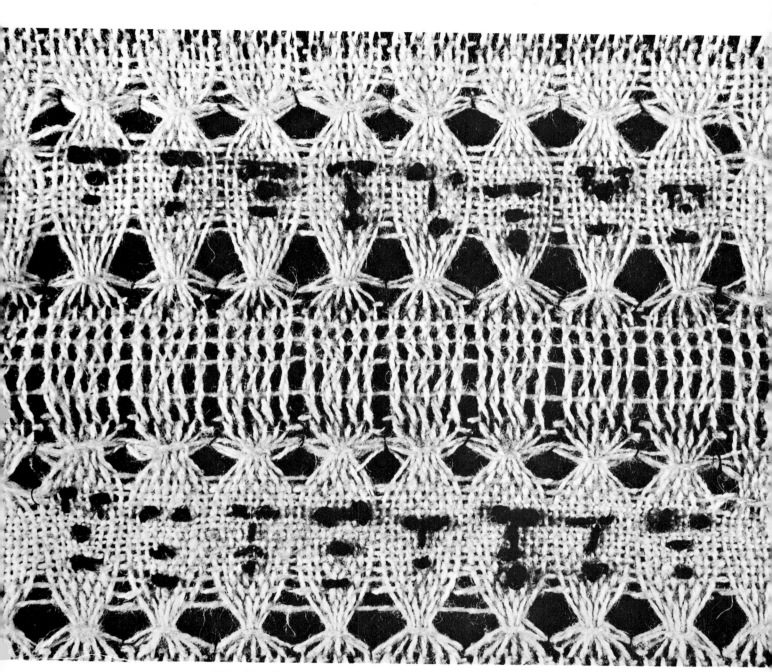

"Many Faces," double weave and leno techniques by Jane Redman.

"Face," double weave by Jane Redman.

"Face," detail of slit tapestry in wool yarns by Jane Redman.
(Photo: John W. Rosenthal)

"Birthday Girl," tapestry weave with many yarns by Ella Earle. (Photo Bob Bailey)

1-1. Simple tools used for weaving: (a) animal bone, (b) and (c) combs for working weft yarns into warp; (d) tapestry bobbin; (e) teasel for brushing woolen fabric to raise a nap.

1

THE WEAVER'S EQUIPMENT

The loom is the weaver's main tool. There are people who insist that it has a personality and will of its own, people who say that an old loom is wise, seasoned, and smooth and that they would never exchange its big beams and stone-weighted reels for modern contraptions. Craftsmen can show you beautiful weaving done on two sticks with yarn stretched between them and a back strap to regulate the tension, and technicians can show you weaving done on big, noisy machines, with one attendant for twenty looms that work with a speed hardly matched by less than an airplane. Birds and spiders use looms provided by nature, without blueprints and without fuss, and handweavers of our time use the same principles to give results that fit their own lives and purposes.

All looms, no matter how diverse, have the same purpose: to create a fabric by interlocking two sets of threads. The threads stretched lengthwise on the loom are called the warp; the crosswise threads interwoven with them are the weft, or filler. The way the warp and weft interlock with each other is the weave or the weave construction.

Many varieties of handlooms are available to the contemporary weaver. They offer simplicity of operation, immediacy of response, smooth, rhythmical motion, and a wide range of design possibilities as reward for careful attention and meticulous craftsmanship in preparing warps and planning patterns.

Choosing a loom and becoming familiar with it can be an exciting experience. It is not my intention to delve into the technical details of every possible kind of handloom, but rather to describe four kinds that I enjoy and that have served my students and myself well for many years. These are the branch loom, the back-strap loom, the table loom, and the foot loom. (For those who wish to explore further, a more complete list of looms is provided in an appendix.)

Before discussing the individual looms, I must briefly take up an elementary subject with which every weaver will sooner or later be confronted: the weaver's vocabulary. The terminology of weaving is indispensable, and it becomes so natural that a conversation between two weavers may sound like the passwords of a secret society to an outsider. The words vary, of course, from language to language, but the meanings are universal technical designations. The most frequently used terms are listed in the Glossary; the reader should become acquainted with them as they are used in the text.

THE BRANCH LOOM

The branch loom is the simplest loom, one that nature provides in never-ending variety. It is, as the name implies, made from the branch of a tree. The natural shape of the branch determines the shape of the finished article because the loom stays connected to the threads and is an integral part of the work. Branch-loom weaving can take the place of flowers in a vase, serve as a centerpiece on a dinner table, float in the air like a mobile, or stand by itself as sculptural form.

A branch loom is chosen for its shape, sturdiness, and size. Any relatively fuzzy yarn will cling to it: wool, cotton, mohair, and novelty yarns are suitable. A length of yarn is tied firmly to the branch with any kind of simple knot and wound back and forth, between and over the twigs, to form the warp. This can make a pleasing work by itself, the effect depending solely on

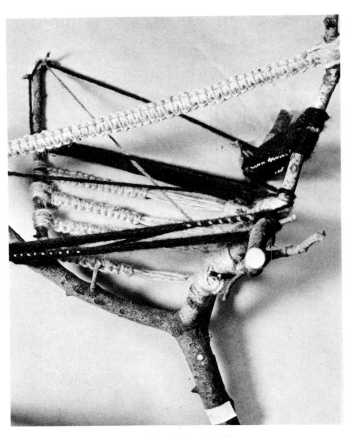

1-2. Branch-loom weaving by Mary Heickman.

1-3. "Tree," branch loom with knotting by Jay Hinz

1-4. Branch-loom weaving by a student.

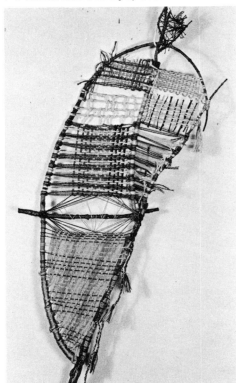

colors and textures of the yarns. Often, however, weft threads are worked over and under the warp threads with a large needle, and the combination of the two sets of threads can yield exciting results. The weave may follow the shape of the branches, build up in solid color stripes, or twist and turn to make small nests and intricate compositions. If the branches are very flexible, as willow branches are, they can be bent to make round forms and spider-web designs—there is no limit to the number of variations imagination can conceive for this simple and delightful form of weaving.

THE BACK-STRAP LOOM

For thousands of years people have done beautiful and complicated weaving on the back-strap loom, which, like the branch loom, is a primitive loom. Its name comes from the belt, made of fiber, cloth, or leather, that is attached to the loom and reaches around the back of the weaver, who thus controls with his body the tension of the warp.

Unlike the branch loom, the back-strap loom requires a shuttle—the device that carries the weft through the warp. The shuttles used with this loom are long flat sticks with a notch at each end on which the weft yarns are wound.

The traveler to Peru, Ecuador, Mexico, or Guatemala can find this traditional loom still in use by Indians. Using the wool of the alpaca and llama from the highlands, or cotton grown in the plains, they produce beautiful blouses, skirts, ponchos, bags, blankets, belts, and ribbons. Even though materials manufactured by fast modern methods may be bought in the store, these weavers continue to work on large back-strap looms with yarns spun on the same wooden spindles their ancestors used, and they beat the weft into place with small, pointed animal bones that are bleached and shiny with age. Dressed in their own colorful fabrics, these weavers create intricate patterns in bright yarns. The very primitiveness of the tool invites a freedom of design that a mechanized loom will not allow.

This most personal of all expression in weaving reached its height in the pre-Columbian textiles, all produced on back-strap looms. The techniques and designs of the period are an inspiration for the contemporary artist. (For the weaver who would like to experience a special joy and sense of achievement, an expert weaver, Madeleine Smith of Windsor, Canada, has written detailed instructions for making and using a back-strap loom. These instructions are included in an appendix.)

1-5. Pattern weaving on a back-strap loom, Guatemala. (Photo Else Regensteiner)

1-6. Pattern weaving on a back-strap loom, Guatemala. (Photo: Else Regensteiner)

1-7. The main parts of a four-harness table loom: (1) breast beam, (2) cloth beam, (3) beater, (4) reed, (5) dents, (6) harnesses, (7) heddles, (8) finger treadles, (9) warp beam, (10) back beam, (11) ratchets with handles, (12) apron and apron rod. (Photo courtesy Structo Division King-Seeley Thermos Co.)

THE TABLE LOOM

It is both valuable and a great satisfaction to understand step by step the operation of the table loom. This small, efficient mechanized loom is fundamentally the same as any larger loom, but it is a simple machine. It is operated with harnesses and finger treadles, which raise the warp threads mechanically. Unlike the foot loom, however, it does not require a permanent tie-up, which would fasten harnesses and treadles together in a set combination. This makes the operation of the loom slower, but it is an advantage for the beginning weaver and designer because the freedom of combining harnesses makes any combination possible simply by a touch of the fingers.

Table looms are constructed of wood or metal and can be purchased in sizes from eight inches to about thirty-six inches in width. They usually have two, four, or eight harnesses, but some are manufactured with as many as twenty-four harnesses for special requirements.

The loom has twelve main parts (see Figure 1-7), each with a special function:

(1) The front or breast beam is the rail over which the warp passes on its way from the reed to the cloth beam.

(2) The cloth beam is the front roller of the loom. The woven fabric is wound on it.

(3) The beater is the swinging beam, holding the reed, that beats the weft into place.

(4) The reed is the steel part, attached to the beater, that spreads the warp. (Even today, on older looms, especially in South American countries, the reed is sometimes made of thin wood slats or reed splinters from which this part got its name.) Reeds are interchangeable and classified by the number of openings (called dents) to an inch. Thus, a number 12 reed is one that has twelve dents to an inch; a number 15 reed, one that has fifteen dents to an inch.

(5) The dents are the open spaces in the reed that

18

1-8. Heddle.

keep each warp thread in its proper place and sequence. The density of the warp is determined by the number of warp threads running through the dents.

(6) The heddles (Figure 1-8) are wires or strings that have an opening or eye in the center through which the warp thread passes.

(7) The harnesses or shafts (made up of heddle frames, heddle bars, and heddles) lift or lower the warp threads.

(8) The treadles, worked by the fingers, are used to manipulate the harnesses.

(9) The warp beam is the back roller to which the warp is attached and on which the warp is wound. It may be either a plain or a sectional roller (one divided into sections by pegs), depending on the method of warping preferred by the weaver. Some looms are equipped with two warp beams, one above the other.

(10) The back beam is the beam over which the warp runs from the heddles to the warp beam.

(11) The ratchets or dogs, which are attached to the cloth beam in front and the warp beam in back, are metal or wooden wheels with teeth into which a pawl, or tongue, falls to hold to warp in tension. They are used to release and tighten the warp as it is moved forward during weaving.

(12) The apron is a piece of fabric or several strong tapes nailed to the cloth beam. The apron holds the apron stick or rod to which the warp is tied, acting as an extension of the beam and preventing the waste of any warp. Another apron is attached to the warp beam.

The warp threads run horizontally, parallel to each other, from the apron in front of the loom through the dents of the reed and then through heddles on alternating harnesses toward the back of the loom, and they are wound in even tension onto the warp beam. As one group of warp threads is lifted by the treadles, the shuttle with the weft wound on it is inserted into the shed—the opening between the two groups of threads—and the interlocking process of weave construction has begun.

Looms with a set of only two harnesses work on the alternating system. As one group of warp threads is lifted, the remaining threads are either lowered or stay stationary, limiting the weave to a simple, basic construction. But the two-harness loom need never yield unimaginative strips of cloth. Its very simplicity is a

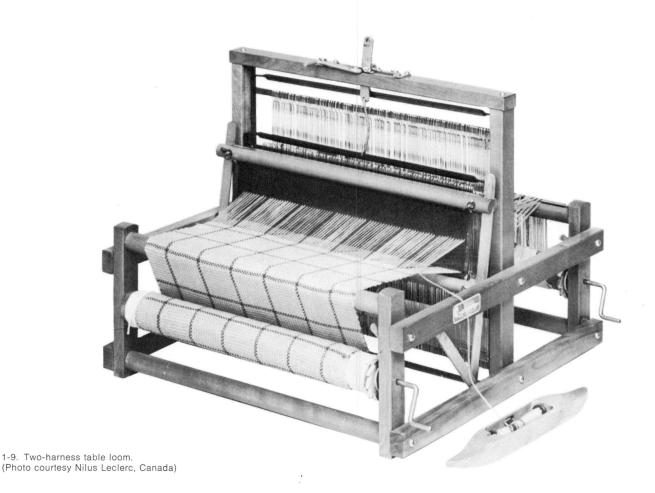

1-9. Two-harness table loom.
(Photo courtesy Nilus Leclerc, Canada)

challenge and incentive for creative variations. Of course, the loom with four harnesses has even wider scope for design, and looms with eight or more harnesses are valuable for the weaver who wants to explore more intricate patterns. The more harnesses a loom has, the more threading and treadling variations are possible.

The table loom is excellent for experimenting and observing the interaction of threading and treadling combinations. However, it is not merely a learning device; it is indispensable for planning a large piece of weaving, and it can produce a variety of finished items, including place mats, scarves, bags, stoles, and even dress material and wall hangings.

THE FOOT LOOM

The foot loom (or foot-power loom) is operated by the weaver's feet, which press down the treadles according to the sequence of the desired pattern. The principal difference between the foot loom and the table loom is the foot treadles. They free the weaver's hands for throwing

1-10. Eight-harness table loom with stand. (Photo courtesy Structo Division King-Seeley Thermos Co.)

1-11. Four-harness counterbalanced foot loom. (Photo courtesy Nilus Leclerc, Canada)

the shuttle and moving the beater, making weaving a faster and more rhythmical process. Directly under each harness is a short horizontal stick called the lam. It is fastened to the harness above and to the treadle below by ropes or chains. This device allows several harnesses to be tied onto one treadle, thereby making many weave combinations possible. A good foot loom will have at least two more treadles than harnesses to allow for a wide range of tie-ups.

There are four principal types of foot loom: the counterbalanced loom, the jack-type loom, the countermarch loom, and the upright loom. There are variations of each of these types, but once a weaver understands the differences between them, he will have no difficulty in using one or another.

The Counterbalanced Loom

The counterbalanced loom was brought to America by early immigrants from Europe, and many fine colonial coverlets and fabrics were woven on it. The name of the loom explains how it works. The counterbalanced

action is accomplished by pulleys or a bar on top of the loom over which the ropes holding the harnesses run. As the treadle is pressed, one group of warp threads is pulled down, while the other group is raised.

Some special characteristics of the counterbalanced loom should be noted: (1) Because the warp threads are lowered when the treadles are pressed, the loom produces a "sinking shed"—one that opens diagonally and is very wide. (2) The loom works smoothly only when the weave is balanced; that is, when an even number of harnesses is raised and lowered simultaneously. (3) The warp must run lengthwise through the center of the reed instead of resting at the base of the dents, as in some other systems. (4) Treadling is easy, and, because of the interaction of the harnesses, does not require much physical effort.

The Jack-Type Loom

The jack-type loom does not need an overhead beam and acts on an entirely different system than the counterbalanced loom. Directly below each harness are two

1-12. The main parts of a four-harness jack-type foot loom: (1) breast beam, (2) cloth beam, (3) beater, (4) reed, (5) dents, (6) harnesses, (7) heddles, (8) foot treadles, (9) warp beam, (10) back beam, (11) ratchet with handle, (12) apron and apron rod, (13) lams, (14) tie-up cords. (Photo courtesy E. E. Gilmore, California)

wooden pieces acting as jack levers that raise the harness when the treadle is pressed. (Some jack-type looms do have an overhead beam, to which the jack levers are connected.) Each of the jack levers is tied to one lam, and the lams in turn are connected to the treadles. As the lam is pulled downward by the treadle, the jack pushes the harness up and lifts its warp threads to an open position. The part of the warp that is not raised stays flat at the base of the reed, resting on a protruding ledge of the beater, called the shuttle race (Figure 1-13).

The jack-type loom has several advantages: (1) Because of the "rising shed" action, each harness can work independently of the others. This makes possible unbalanced weaves. (2) Double weaves, honeycomb weaves, block weaves, and many other single and combination tie-ups can be made easily. (3) Because the lower part of the shed stays flat on the shuttle race, the shuttle is not apt to fall between the warp threads to the floor as it slides through the warp. (4) Harness frames on most jacktype looms lift out of their grooves easily for changing or entering heddles, as needed. (It is best to lay these frames on a table and transfer the heddles with the help of a flexible transfer rod, provided with some looms by the manufacturer.)

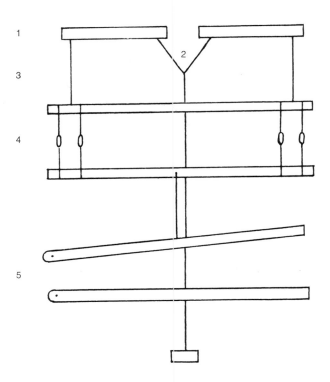

1-14. How the countermarch loom works: (1) overhead beam, (2) jack lever, (3) ropes, (4) harness with heddles, (5) lams.

1-13. Shuttle race. (Photo courtesy Nilus Leclerc, Canada)

The Countermarch Loom

The countermarch (or contramarche) loom, frequently called a double tie-up loom, combines the action of the jack-type loom with the action of the counterbalanced loom. Its main characteristic is two sets of lams, placed horizontally under the harnesses, one below the other. It often has many harnesses and huge overhead beams, and sometimes a bench is built into its frame. As a harness is raised by one set of lams, the rest of the harnesses are pulled down by the second set. This system is very effective because it gives an excellent shed (which allows the use of especially large shuttles) and an unbalanced number of harnesses can be raised.

As weavers are sometimes puzzled by the countermarch loom, I want to explain the tie-up as clearly as possible. There is a jack arrangement for each harness on top of the upper loom frame. These are called overhead jacks. Each harness is individually connected with its own jack by ropes on each side of its frame. There are two sets of lams below the harnesses, one set above the other. The horizontal sticks of the upper lams are shorter than on the lower lams, and are called the short set. The horizontal sticks on the lower lams are called the long set. Each harness frame is connected directly with its lam from the short set. This controls the sinking shed. Each lam from the long set is connected to its overhead jack by long ropes that run between the harnesses. This controls the rising shed. Both the rising and the sinking sheds are operated at the same time

1-15. Irene J. Tsosie, Navajo weaver from St. Michaels, Arizona, working on an upright loom.

Below:
1-16. Contemporary two-harness upright loom. (Photo courtesy Nilus Leclerc, Canada)

by the same treadle. As some of the warp threads are pulled up, the other warp threads are pulled down. For this reason, both groups must be tied to one treadle. The effort of tying two sets of lams to harnesses and treadles is considerable, but once the tie-up is in place, large pieces can be woven very easily, and this is the main reason the countermarch loom is used.

The Upright Loom

Huge upright looms are very often used for rug and tapestry weaving. Knotted pile rugs, looped rugs, and thick flat carpets, as well as many kinds of tapestry, can be woven on the vertical warp of the upright loom.

The primitive upright loom, which may still be seen in South American countries, consists of a rectangular frame of four beams put into the ground or fastened to a wooden base. The warp runs vertically, often as a single continuous thread, around the top and bottom horizontal beams. Separation of odd and even threads is accomplished by a wooden rod fastened to the vertical frame at a convenient height. String heddles, or leashes, are used to pull up the opposite groups of warp threads. As weaving progresses, the warp moves around the top and bottom beams in a continuous ellipse, and the material can therefore be woven twice the size of the frame.

Contemporary weavers who wish to work on a small-scale upright loom may look to the American Indian for guidance and inspiration. The Navajos weave intricate

and beautiful designs using string heddles and flat pick-up sticks as the only help in raising the warps.

Foot treadles and harnesses have been added in the modern version of the upright loom. This loom preserves the vertical warp but has several efficient new features. Rollers on top and bottom serve as warp and cloth beams. The harnesses with metal heddles move forward and backward in horizontal motion, activated by their tie-up to the two foot treadles underneath. A beater and reed spread the warp evenly, speeding the weaving whenever the type of work permits their use. However, the same loom can be turned into a loom without harnesses and beater by the simple process of turning it around and using only the top and bottom beams to hold the warp. In this case rod and string heddles may be attached, as on a primitive upright loom, and the foot treadles may be ignored.

The upright loom, far from being outmoded, is one of the most versatile tools available to the handweaver today. It lends itself not only to rugs and tapestries but also to wall hangings in all forms and shapes. It gives a full view of the work in progress from front and back, and, whether it is a simple four-beamed frame or a more complicated two-harness foot-treadle loom, it is an excellent supplement to any horizontal loom a weaver may possess.

1-17. Tapestry being woven on an upright loom by Darlyne Kasper.

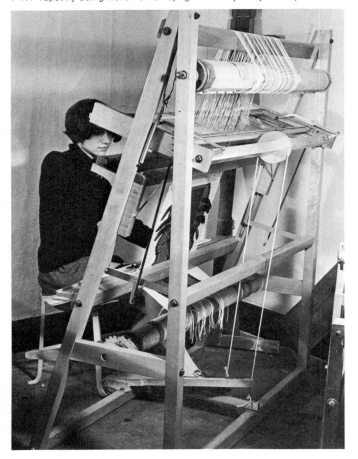

OTHER EQUIPMENT

While the loom is the weaver's basic tool, some additional equipment is also necessary.

The Loom Bench

It is important to use a stool or bench that is high enough for weaving on table looms or foot looms without straining the back, shoulders, arms, or knees. Good benches have a slanting seat (the higher edge faces the front of the loom). Some have a sliding drawer that extends the full length of the bench; this can be used as a shelf while weaving and for storage. Others have for a seat a wooden lid that opens on hinges, uncovering some storage space underneath. A few looms are specially designed for use with an ordinary chair.

1-18. Loom bench with drawer.

Shuttles

There are different kinds of shuttles: stick shuttles, rug shuttles, and boat shuttles. Which shuttle the weaver should use is determined by the size of the loom, the depth of the shed, the width of the warp, and the texture of the weft yarns. Some materials are woven with one shuttle only, but for others several shuttles are used in rotation.

The flat stick shuttle is suited for weaving narrow samples and for use with table looms, since small amounts of yarn can be wound on as needed, and the shuttle can be put through a shallow shed. Stick shuttles come in various sizes or can be made in any convenient length from fiberboard, strong cardboard, or wooden slats. They must be strong enough not to bend and smooth enough not to catch on the warp threads. The yarn is wound lengthwise from end to end. A notch at each end holds it securely in place; the beginning end is fastened with a loop to one of the notches. As weaving proceeds, a sufficient length of the weft yarn has to be unwound each time the shuttle is inserted into the shed.

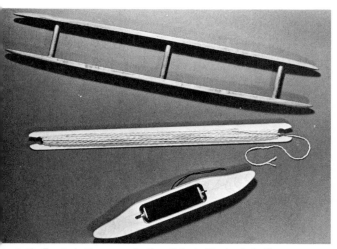

1-19. Top to bottom: rug shuttle, stick shuttle, boat shuttle.

1-20. Boat shuttle with slippery yarn on bobbin.

Bobbins

Bobbins should fit correctly and easily into the hollow of the boat shuttle. Bobbins may be bought ready made in plastic or wood or fashioned by the weaver himself from brown wrapping paper or even newspaper. Commercially manufactured bobbins have rims that prevent the yarn from sliding over the edges, but homemade bobbins, called quills, correctly wound, can serve a weaver just as well. As with all steps of weaving, attention to detail is essential to the learning process. To gradually acquire skill even in the small task of winding a bobbin is an enjoyable experience, and marks the difference between good and poor craftsmanship.

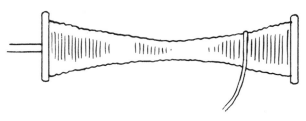

1-21. Plastic bobbins with rims, wound correctly.

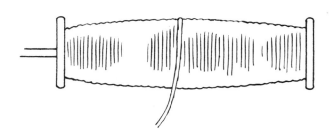

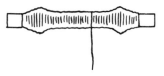

1-22. Cardboard or paper quills, wound correctly.

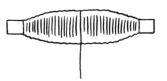

The rug shuttle or throw shuttle is a larger version of the stick shuttle. It consists of two flat wood pieces that form sides and two small dowels that connect them. This kind of shuttle, which may range in length from eight inches to eighteen inches, accommodates heavy yarns and is most frequently used for weaving rugs and sturdy upholstery fabric.

The graceful boat shuttle is the most useful and the weaver's favorite. Fine or medium threads are wound on a bobbin that is inserted on a spindle in the hollow part of the shuttle, which very much resembles a wooden rowboat. The yarn from the bobbin is carried through a slit in the curved side and unwinds continuously while the shuttle glides through the shed. This shuttle is by far the speediest device for rhythmical weaving, and the weaver soon learns to use it with alternating hands and an easy flip of the wrist.

In rare cases when two different threads are to be woven together simultaneously in the same shed, a shuttle that holds two bobbins may be used. This shuttle has two hollow compartments, each with a slit on the side.

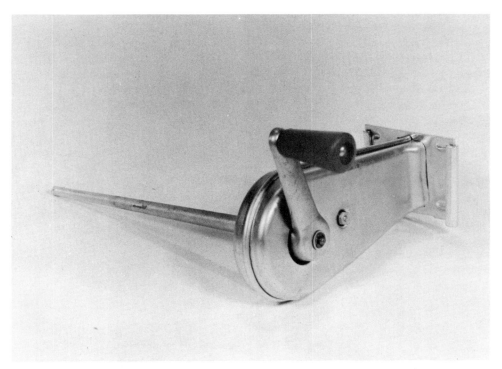

1-23. Wall-type bobbin winder. (Photo courtesy Structo Division, King-Seeley Thermos Co.)

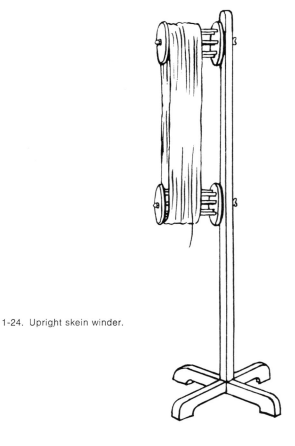

1-24. Upright skein winder.

Bobbin Winders

A winder is needed to wind the yarn on the bobbin. It consists of a spindle driven by a wheel that is turned by hand or electrically. The best winders have a spindle tapered to fit different sizes of bobbins or quills. Many busy weavers prefer a winder driven by a small motor that is regulated with the same kind of foot pedal commonly used for electric sewing machines.

The method of working the winder is the same whatever kind is used. The winder is clamped to a table top or screwed to a wall. The bobbin, with the beginning end of the thread tied to it, is pushed onto the spindle. The thread, unwinding from a skein, spool, or cone, is held under tension with one hand. As the spindle turns, the thread is wound onto it. If the bobbin has rims, the yarn is guided back and forth; if there are no rims, as in homemade quills, the yarn is built up by winding a "bump" on each side and then filling in the center (see Figures 1-21 and 1-22). No more yarn should be wound on a bobbin than the shuttle can hold easily.

Skein Winders

Skein winders speed up the winding process considerably. Upright models have two rollers that can be adjusted to the length of the skein and turn as the yarn is unwound. Table winders, which fold up like an umbrella and are clamped to a table top, can be used if floor space is limited.

1-25. Spool rack.

1-26. Threading hook.

Spool Racks

A good spool rack is indispensable for warping, or putting a warp on the loom. The spool rack needed depends on the method of warping used. A large spool rack is needed for the sectional method; a smaller one is sufficient for chain warping. (Both chain warping and sectional warping are discussed fully in Chapter 3).

Warping Boards and Trees

The warping board or frame is a device for measuring warp yarn for chain warping. It is a strong wooden board that has pegs to hold the yarn and to keep the threads in the right order (see Figure 3-5a and b). A warping board can be used when the warp is from five to ten yards long, but generally will not hold more than ten yards.

For longer chain warps, a warping tree is used (see Figure 3-6). The warp yarn does not have to be guided but only held by hand because the tree swivels on its base, so the warp is wound on four sides of the frame. Pegs at the top and bottom keep the threads in order.

Warp Tensioners

In sectional warping, a tensioner is necessary for rolling sections of warp from the spools onto the warp beam (see Figure 3-22). The tensioner keeps the warp yarns in even tension and in the right order.

Threading Hooks

The threading or reed hook is a flat, narrow rod that has a notch at one end and a wooden or plastic handle. It is used to pull the warp threads through the reed and heddles.

Yardage Counters

In sectional warping, a commercial yardage counter is useful for counting the yards of yarn to be wound on the spools.

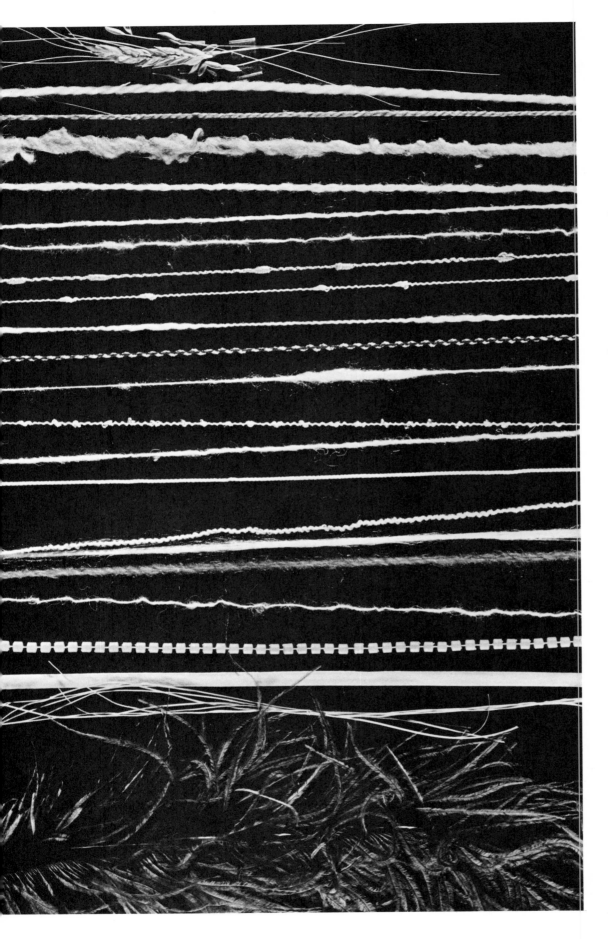

loosely spun natural wool
jute

handspun wool

two-ply wool yarn

three-ply cotton yarn

brushed mohair yarn

cotton and metallic nub yarn

novelty yarn (nub or knop yarn)

mercerized cotton flake

novelty yarn (bouclé)

novelty yarn (flake)

novelty yarn (ratiné)
handspun wool

three-ply nylon yarn

wool ratiné

silk floss

wool and nylon blend

handspun dog hair

plastic beads

cellophane

reed

feather

2-1. A variety of weaving materials

2

YARNS

Two basic terms, fiber and filament, are used to describe yarns. A filament is a long continuous thread, like those spun by the spider or silkworm or produced synthetically. A fiber is a short length of the basic material, and several are usually spun together to make a yarn.

Choosing yarns is the most interesting preliminary step to weaving, for the tactile and visual pleasures of the material blend in weaving as in no other medium. Since it is possible to work with nearly any long and straight material, the variety that is available is overwhelming. Yarns of every color, texture, and size are manufactured, and the weaver of today can order samples from all over the world. Handspinners have discovered anew the beauty of natural wools, the softness of llama and alpaca, the warmth of cashmere, and the unique sheen of mohair. Many weavers turn to spinning and spinners to weaving to complement their various experiences.

For the beginning weaver the most auspicious way to start is to collect yarns, even if at first in small amounts. To lay them on the table in colorful array and observe how they look together, how they feel, how one complements another is a valuable beginning experience that combines playing with testing and learning with designing. Such immediate experimentation encourages enthusiasm and the creative spirit; after the student has glimpsed the wealth of possibilities available to him, he will be eager to learn the qualities and origins of fibers. To anticipate the behavior of fibers in the final product, it is necessary to have a basic understanding of their different properties. These properties include staple length (the average length of a group of fibers), diameter, color, texture, luster, elasticity, tensile strength, resistance to abrasion, wear, and sunlight, affinity for dyes, etc.

There are two main groups of fibers—natural and man-made, or synthetic. Synthetic yarns are often very fine and therefore impractical for handweaving; the handweaver uses them mainly as an addition to natural fibers and in comparatively coarse sizes. The handweaver has a special attachment to natural fibers, which have more life and give more tactile satisfaction than their man-made counterparts. The natural fibers include animal fibers, vegetable fibers, and mineral fibers.

ANIMAL FIBERS

2-2. Sheep.

Wool

Wool is the fiber from the fleece of the sheep. Its quality varies with the many different types and breeds of sheep, as well as with the part of the body from which the fleece comes. There are two categories of raw wool, based on its intended use: apparel wool, made from the longest and finest fibers, and carpet wool.

The outside of the fiber is made up of flat, irregular scales that overlap each other, giving the fiber elasticity. Some fibers are fine, some coarse; and some are long, some short. Fine wool fibers range from about two and a half inches to five inches in length, have about 2,400 scales to an inch, and are about 1/2,000 of an inch in diameter. Only pure Merino sheep or breeds with predominantly Merino blood produce fibers classified as fine wools.

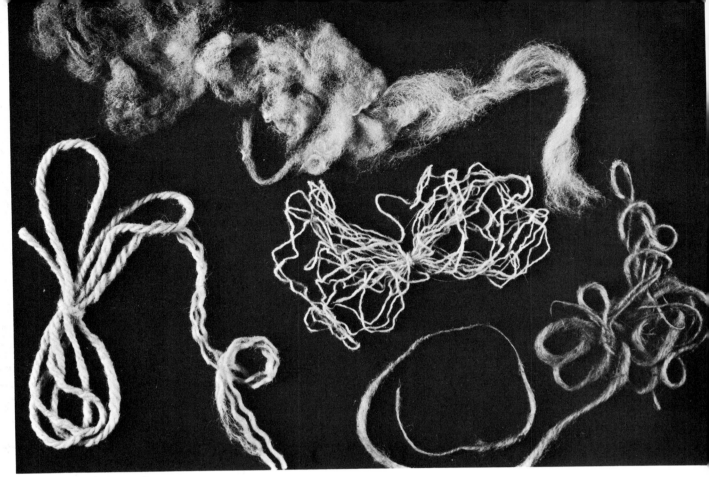

2-3. Raw wool and spun wool.

2-4. Primitive spindles for spinning wool and cotton fibers.

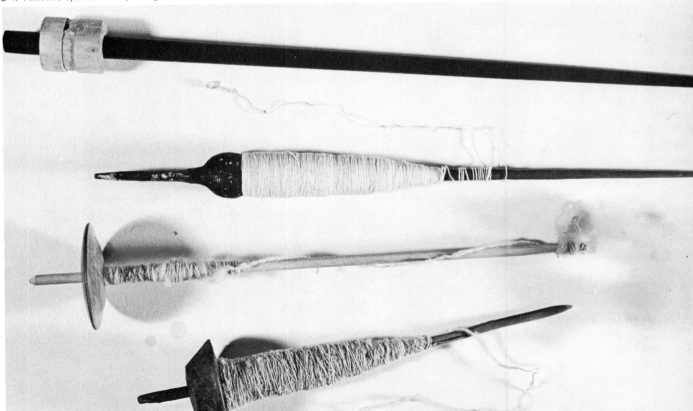

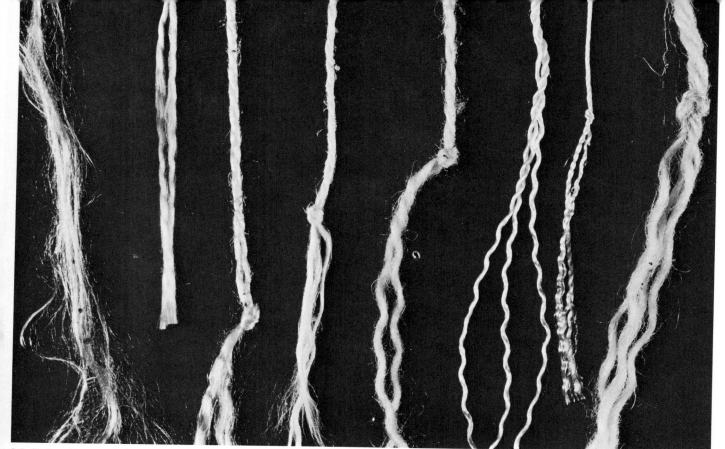

2-5. Various fibers made into two- and three-ply yarns.

The first fleece sheared from a lamb, when it is about six or eight months old, is called lamb's wool, first clip, or fleece wool. Sheep are generally shorn once a year. The shearer works with electric clippers, removing the whole fleece in one piece. An expert can shear as many as two hundred sheep in a day. The fleece is sent to the mill in bales ranging from three hundred to a thousand pounds, depending upon the country. It is then sorted by experienced men who can determine the quality by quick touch. As many as twenty distinct grades may be obtained from one fleece, the grade being determined by type, length, fineness, elasticity, and strength of the fiber. The finest wool comes from the shoulders and the sides; wool from the lower part of the back is of good quality, while that from the tail and legs, called britch wool, is stiff, straight, and coarse.

The sorted wool is scoured to remove animal grease and dirt. (The grease or oil that is washed out constitutes 40 to 60 percent of the wool's weight and is one of its most important by-products, lanolin.) However, since the loss of oil makes the wool brittle, animal, vegetable, or mineral oil must be added before the next step, when the wool is carded, a process that can be compared to brushing or combing the fur of a dog or cat. Large brushes with wire bristles are used to remove remaining bits of burrs and twigs and to disentangle the fiber bunches. The process leaves the wool smooth and fluffy, and ready to be made into roving— a rope of wool suitable for spinning into yarn.

From this point on, the processing differs depending on whether the end product is to be woolen or worsted yarn. Woolen yarns are spun from the shorter fibers directly after carding and have a soft, fuzzy texture. Worsted yarns are made only from the best, finest, and longest fibers, which, after the carding process, are combed until all the fibers lie parallel.

The spinning process twists the fibers into a continous yarn, called single ply. They can be spun with only a few twists per inch (soft-twisted yarns) or with many twists (hard-twisted yarns). The fibers can be spun from left to right, which produces a Z twist, or from right to left, an S twist. Two, three, or four singles twisted together after spinning make two-ply, three-ply, or four-ply yarn. When the yarns are plied together, they are twisted in the direction opposite to their own twist, which keeps the strands interlocked.

In its natural state, wool ranges from white through gray and brown to black. When wool is dyed before spinning, it is called stock or fleece dyed. Heather tweed yarns, which combine several colors, are produced by spinning stock-dyed fibers together. If the wool is dyed after spinning, it is called skein dyed. When dyed after weaving, it is called piece dyed.

After carding, roving, spinning, and, usually, dyeing, the wool is ready for weaving. Wool yarn is flexible, has excellent tensile strength, and is very elastic. Its elasticity makes it wrinkle resistant, but also causes a high percentage of shrinkage. Wool fabric is very absorbent (a dry piece can absorb 30 percent of its weight in moisture without feeling damp and up to 50 percent without becoming saturated), and it is an excellent insulator.

In the United States, three classes of wool have been defined by the Wool Products Labeling Act, which is meant to protect the consumer by clearly stating the content of woolen fabrics. However, the label does not show the grade of the wool fiber. "Wool" or "virgin wool" means wool that has never been processed in any way before being manufactured into the finished product. The best fabrics are always made of virgin wool. "Reprocessed wool" is made from woven, knitted, or felted fabrics that have never been used, such as mill ends or scraps from the cutting tables of tailors. The fibers are broken up and completely reprocessed, thereby losing some of their original qualities but retaining enough to permit the manufacture of serviceable fabrics. "Reused wool" is made from rags, clothing, or other used wool products. The rags are cleaned and sorted according to type; then they are shredded into fiber and chemically processed. Reused wool is nearly always blended with some stronger new wool and is used in a wide range of utility fabrics. Frequently, identical garments are manufactured in all three qualities. The difference is noticeable not only in the price of the article but also in the "feel of hand" of the fabric. Of course, the label must also state the percentage of other fibers added to the wool.

The weaver can estimate the yardage in a pound of yarn once he understands the meaning of the important term "yarn count" and learns the standard by which diverse yarns are measured. The count of worsted is based on the standard of 560 yards spun from a pound of raw wool; that is, a number 1 worsted yarn has 560 yards per pound, and a number 2 yarn has twice as many yards—1,120—per pound. The count of woolen yarn is based on two separate systems. The "cut" system uses a base of 300 yards to the cut, making 300 yards per pound of raw wool the standard for a number 1 single yarn. In the "American run" system, which is generally used, 1,600 yards per pound of raw wool is the standard count for a number 1 yarn. The higher the number of the yarn, the finer it is spun and the more yardage it has.

When yarn is plied, the number of yards in a pound is reduced accordingly.

Specialty Fibers

Specialty, or hair, fibers are classified as wool but come from animals other than sheep. These fibers are used alone or in combination with sheep's wool for added warmth, lighter weight, and luxurious softness. The finest of them come from the hair of the animals' soft inner coat.

2-6. Camel.

Camel Hair

The most widely used and best known specialty fiber comes from the two-humped Bactrian camel, bred in Asia. The hair is obtained by shearing or plucking the animal or by collecting the hair that falls off during the shedding period. Camel hair is generally used in its natural colors of tan or reddish brown, and it makes beautiful coats, shawls, and other wearing apparel.

Llama

The llama is a native of the high Andes Mountains in Ecuador, Peru, Bolivia, and Argentina. It is said that llamas were the basis of the Inca economy, furnishing the Indians with food and transportation as well as clothing. Long before the Inca period, however, beautiful fabrics were woven from the lightweight, lustrous fiber. Llama fleece is obtained by shearing. Its color ranges from white to brown and black. The yarn is used to make ponchos, and high-quality fabrics that are durable and extremely warm.

2-7. Alpaca.

Alpaca

The alpaca is a smaller relative of the llama. Staple length of its fine hair is between eight and sixteen inches, but if permitted to grow beyond the biennial shearing, the fleece may reach thirty-six inches in length. The rarest breed of alpaca, the suri, has even finer and longer hair. When alpaca fleece is sorted, a variety of colors is obtained, including white, fawn, gray, light brown, dark or reddish brown, black, and spotted.

Vicuña

Smaller than the llama and alpaca, to which it is related, the vicuña is a graceful and elusive creature that lives only in the highest peaks of the Andes, at altitudes of 12,500 to 16,000 feet. It has never been domesticated, but the Incas, unlike modern man, rounded up and corraled the animals for shearing and then set them free. Today, ruthless hunting and killing of the vicuñas has diminished their population and limited the supply of the fiber so it does not play a major role in the world market. Efforts are being made to enforce conservation laws to save the species from extinction.

2-8. Goat.

Mohair

Mohair comes from the long-haired Angora goat, originally a native of Turkey, but now raised in South Africa and the southwestern United States.

Mohair is graded according to the age of the goat and the type of fleece—tight lock, flat lock, or fluff. Tight lock is considered the best. Kid and adult hairs differ in fineness and strength, and the best-quality mohair apparel fabrics use only kid hairs.

Because it has less crimp than sheep's wool, mohair has a relatively smooth surface. It is therefore very lustrous and spins into a thin yarn, which can be brushed to give a soft and luxurious finish. Mohair also has many of the qualities of sheep's wool—warmth, resilience, and wearability. It takes dyes well, and is wrinkle resistant. Mohair is used primarily in apparel, rugs, and upholstery fabric.

Cashmere

In the Himalaya Mountains, in Tibet, India, and China, lives the Kashmir goat. The goats with the finest fleece are found at the highest altitudes. The fine inner hair of the animals must be obtained by combing, since they will not permit clipping or shearing. In combing, many long dark hairs come out, and these must be separated by hand, a long and tedious process. No matter how much care is used, some of the long hair remains in the fleece, and this is a characteristic of cashmere yarn.

The natural color of cashmere varies from pure white to gray or brownish gray. The quantity of white fleece is small—20 percent of the total. Cashmere is used to make luxurious wearing apparel and has special appeal because of its soft touch, light weight, and excellent warmth.

Besides hair fibers from the camel and goat families, fibers from animals such as beaver, chinchilla, and angora rabbit as well as other fur-bearing animals such as fox, weasel, mink, and even dog are sometimes added to wool for softness and textural interest.

Silk

The history of silk began in ancient China. Many legends are told of its discovery and development. According to one, an emperor's young consort who had many mulberry trees in her garden by chance unraveled the fine filament of a silkworm's cocoon, finding that by dropping the cocoon into hot water, the gummy substance holding it together could be dissolved and a long thread wound off. Another empress, Hsi-ling-shi, wife of Huang-ti (2640 B.C.), is said to have personally cared for silkworms and to have made silk fabric fashionable in China.

However discovered, the process of silk production became a carefully guarded state secret, not revealed to the West until the time of the Emperor Justinian, the sixth century A.D. From then on, silk raising, or sericulture, and silk weaving spread through Europe, and silk fabrics and garments have remained the ultimate in beauty and elegance to modern times.

The life cycle of the silk moth is fascinating. Each moth lays between three hundred and eight hundred eggs. These hatch in three days to a week, and the silkworms, each about an eighth of an inch long, gnaw their way out. They must then be carefully tended and continuously fed with fresh dry young mulberry leaves. Only silkworms raised on mulberry leaves produce the finest silk; those fed on oak or other trees are considered wild and produce brown filaments, called tussah silk.

Silkworms eat voraciously and grow rapidly, increasing their weight many times and reaching a length of about three inches. They are fully grown after thirty days. The crunching sound of their chewing ceases; they attach themselves by their own guy lines to straw or twigs, and start spinning themselves into their cocoons. The silkworm makes more than one movement of its head a second to build up the cocoon, spinning it back and forth in a figure eight. The worm has two vessels near its head: one contains the silk, the other the gummy substance called sericin. Both vessels are united by a spinneret that leads to a small orifice below the mouth from which the two substances flow as one filament.

The cocoons are hard oval shells, finished in two or three days. Then the worms change into chrysalises and become moths in about fifteen days. Since pierced cocoons from which moths have emerged cannot be reeled off into a continuous filament, only the moths needed for breeding are allowed to emerge. These die as soon as they have mated and laid their eggs, and

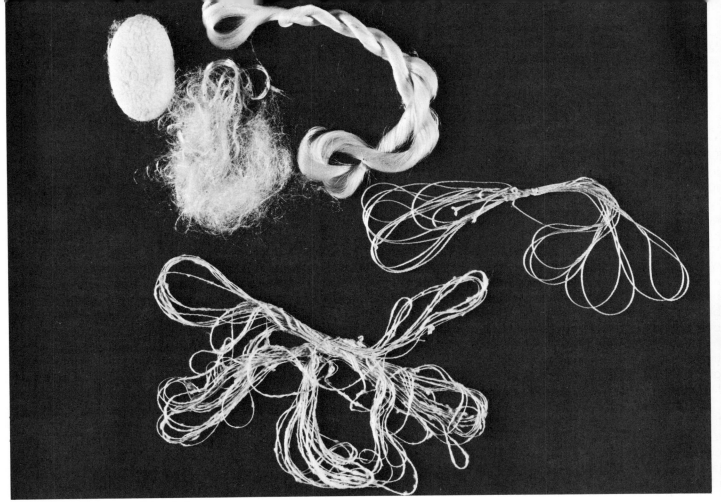

2-9. Silk: cocoon, filament, skein, plied yarn, spun yarn.

their cocoons, together with those made by two worms (douppioni) are put aside. The other chrysalises are killed in the cocoon by hot dry air, and the cocoons are processed.

Each cocoon yields between 500 and 1,600 yards of silk, but only part of each cocoon can be reeled. Several cocoons are dropped into boiling water to soften the sericin and loosen the filaments. The ends of the filaments are then caught, unwound, and reeled together, making a smooth and fine uniform thread. This is raw silk. Later the raw silk is twisted, in a process called throwing, and sometimes it is plied. Finally, the silk yarn is wound into skeins or put on tubes or cones. Silk made from the pierced cocoons and douppioni must be spun. This yarn produces uneven and nubby-textured fabric (also called douppioni). Douppioni and tussah silk can be combined.

The most important quality of silk is its extreme fineness together with great tensile strength: a filament of silk is stronger than a steel wire of the same diameter. Silk has a lovely natural sheen, and it can be blended successfully with other fibers such as wool or linen.

The fineness of reeled silk yarn is measured by the denier system. The denier system dates from the sixteenth century, when a king of France revived the use of a coin (the *denarius*) first minted by Julius Caesar. The French king, Francis I, established the denier as standard weight for measuring silk and is known as the father of the silk industry.

Two different systems are applied, one for reeled silk, the other for spun silk. When 450 meters (about 492.2 yards) of a reeled silk thread weigh one denier (D)—.05 grams—the silk is a number 1 yarn. There are 4,464,528 yards in one pound of a number 1 denier silk; to find the number of yards in a pound of a certain silk, divide the denier number into 4,464,528. In contrast to other systems, in deniers, the higher the number, the coarser the yarn and the less yardage per pound.

Because silk is a natural filament, it varies in size. For this reason, two numbers are given to indicate the denier size, and a 13/15 D thread, for example, means a thread between these two sizes.

For spun silk, the yardage is computed on the basis of the number of hanks of 840 yards each needed to make a pound of yarn. The number of plies does not affect the count: the yardage in a given number yarn stays the same whether the yarn is plied or not. Thus, a number 30 single-ply silk yarn has thirty times 840, or 25,200 yards per pound; a two-ply (2/30) silk yarn also has 25,200 yards per pound, because two single number 60 strands have been plied to make it.

VEGETABLE FIBERS

2-10. Cotton boll.

Cotton

Cotton has long been a basic fabric fiber—it was used in India as early as 5000 B.C. The cotton plant belongs to the mallow family, related to hollyhock and hibiscus. It grows only in warm climates. The seeds are planted early in the spring. In about two months, the plants appear and grow into a low bushy plant about four feet in height. In a few weeks buds begin to form, and three weeks later blossoms appear. The flowers open, wither, and fall off, leaving the small pod known as the cotton boll. When ripe, about two months later, the fluffy white bolls burst open and the cotton inside them is ready to be picked.

The first step in the production of cotton is to separate the seeds from the lint, a process done by the cotton gin. The lint is cleaned and packed into bales of about five hundred pounds.

The next step is carding—the cotton is cleaned and the fibers are separated by machine and formed into a rope called a sliver. Several slivers are combined and compressed into one, by drawing, after which the cotton is combed. The process, comparable to the treatment of worsted yarns, produces the best-quality cotton.

Then the cotton is made into roving, a smaller and slightly twisted strand. Cotton yarn is spun from roving.

Cotton yarn or finished cotton products are frequently mercerized—a process of immersion in a caustic-soda solution—which makes the fiber stronger, more lustrous, and more receptive to dyes.

The quality of cotton depends on several factors. One is the staple length of the fiber: staple of less than one inch produces a coarser fabric; medium and long staple fibers—one to one and an eighth inches—are the most common in American textiles. Fine cotton, which has a smooth, almost silky texture, is woven from extra-long staple. In the United States, cotton is rated from "Good Middling" (the highest quality) to "Good Ordinary."

The standard for the yardage count of cotton is 840 yards per pound. Thus, a number 1 cotton has 840 yards per pound; a number 30 yarn has thirty times as many yards per pound. When two number 30 threads are plied together, the resulting yarn is a 30/2 yarn, which has half the yardage per pound.

No other fiber has quite the versatility and wearability of cotton. It takes well to a wide range of dyes and bleaches, washes with ease, responds beautifully to many finishes, withstands changes of temperature and humidity, and is nonirritating to the skin. It blends well with man-made fibers. For these qualities, the wide range of cotton yarns available is of special interest to the weaver.

2-11. Cotton: boll, raw cotton, roving, spun and plied yarn.

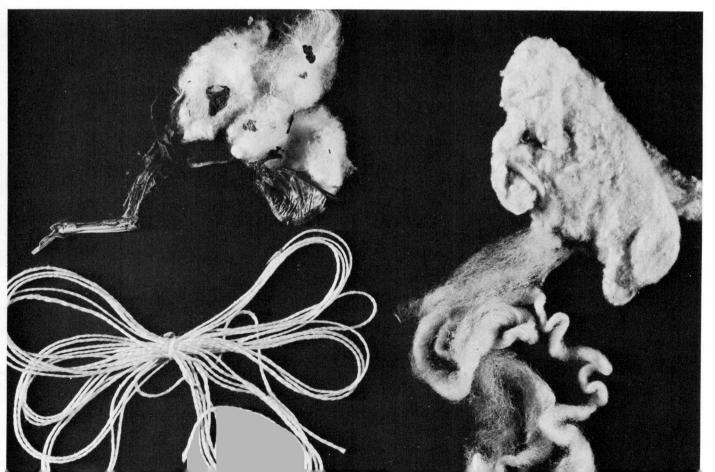

Bast Fibers

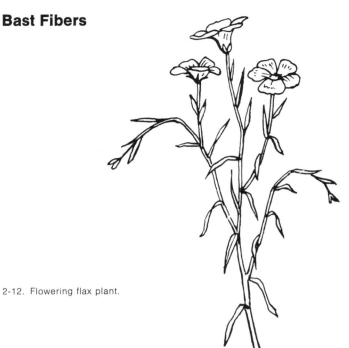

2-12. Flowering flax plant.

Linen

No bast fiber has a wider range of uses than linen, the fiber of the flax plant. Linen is considered the most ancient of textile fibers, predating even cotton.

Flax is grown from seeds planted close together so that the plants grow long stalks, branching only at the top. Because the fiber extends down to the roots, the plants must be pulled up for harvesting. The fibrous stalks are retted—soaked in pure, clear water to rot away the woody core and dissolve the gums that hold the fibers together. Then the fibers are dried and sent to the mill, where the woody stalks are separated from the desired fiber by a process called scutching. The fibers are hackled (cleaned and straightened by combing), carded, drawn, and spun into yarn. Two types of yarn are made. Short fibers are spun into irregular yarn, called tow; the longest fibers are combed and spun into strong, smooth yarn called line.

Flax is composed largely of cellulose, which makes a smooth fiber with good luster. Although it is not elastic and therefore linen fabric wrinkles easily, it is strong, and it has good natural color, high absorbency, and washability.

The yardage count of linen is based on the lea, a unit of three hundred yards, spun from one pound of raw flax.

Jute

Jute comes from the stalk of a plant that originated in the Mediterranean region and was transplanted to India and East Pakistan, which are today its largest producers. The jute plant averages ten to fifteen feet in height; its

2-13. Linen yarn, flax fiber, tow linen.

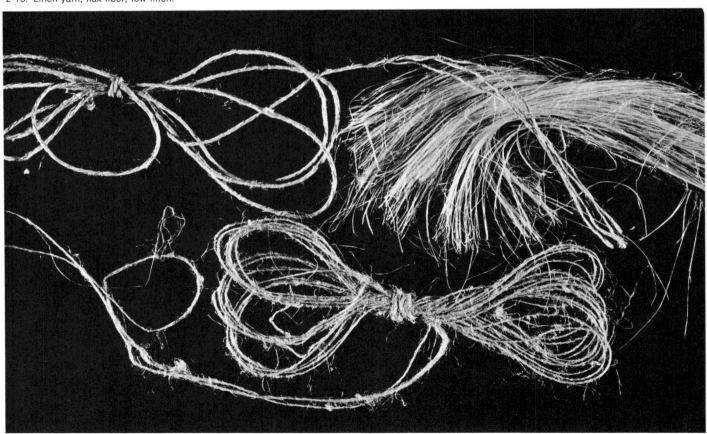

fibers range from four to seven feet in length and are prepared like linen by cleaning (rippling), retting, scutching, and hackling.

Jute fiber is strong and lustrous. It is yellow-brown in color, but it can be bleached and dyed. Although it tends to disintegrate in water and has poor elasticity, it is being used increasingly for bags, cords, burlap, wall coverings, and apparel cloth because of its good tactile qualities.

Hemp

Hemp, like linen, is an ancient textile fiber. There are many different kinds of plant known as hemp, but the best-known varieties are grown in the Philippines (Manila hemp) and Africa (bowstring hemp).

Ramie

Ramie, known also as China grass, is obtained from the stalk of a nettle plant. It grows from five to eight feet high, and its fiber has an average length of five to six inches. The fiber is white and has an excellent resistance to bacteria and mildew. It is absorbent, it dries quickly, and it is extremely strong.

Production of ramie yarn is limited because it is hard to process. Newly discovered methods for growing it, separating the fibers, and spinning have resulted in a larger but still limited output. Ramie is used mainly for apparel fabrics, alone and blended with other fibers, for fishnets, canvas, and filter cloths and other industrial fabrics.

Less Known Bast Fibers

Sunn, kenaf, and urena are bast fibers grown and used in small amounts and only seldom available to handweavers.

Some fibers used for weaving are obtained from barks and leaves. Abaca is one of the best known. It is a lustrous leaf fiber, taken from the outer layer of the leaf sheath of the Musa plant. Most abaca comes from and is woven in the Philippines and is known to us from finely textured place mats and woven baskets.

Sisal and henequen are agave fibers. They are similar to abaca and can be drawn into strands forty to fifty inches long. They are used primarily for rope and twine, and they have a rough, natural texture that is intriguing to handweavers.

Pineapple fibers, which come from the leaves of the plant, are little known but produce some of the finest and most delicate fabrics. Used mostly in the Philippines, cloth woven from pineapple fibers is soft, luxurious, flexible, and strong. The fibers are sometimes combined with silk.

The handweaver is fortunate in that he can use many plants directly from the field or tree, in addition to processed fibers and yarns. Stalks of dried plants and flowers, twigs, and grasses can be woven very successfully, as illustrated in Figures 2-14, 2-15, and 2-16.

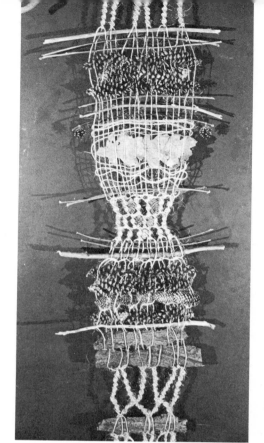

2-14. Wall hanging made with linen yarn, pine cones, dried leaves, and wood by Carolyn Saberniak.

2-15. Place mat woven with wood and bamboo by Helen Little.

2-16. A medley of yarns and pebbles makes an interesting texture in this piece by Helga Zirkel.

MINERAL FIBERS

Asbestos

Asbestos is a mineral fiber—a fiber with no cell structure. It can be made into yarn and spun and woven like cotton or wool. Its most important property is, of course, its complete resistance to heat and fire.

Glass Fiber

From a heated glass marble, a thin fiber can be drawn and by fast rotation made into a fine thread. Fiber glass is fireproof; it resists stains and does not fade; it can be washed without ironing, and takes dyes successfully. It is used for curtains and insulation material. However, small particles may rub off in use, and some handweavers are allergic to it.

Metallic Fibers

Metallic fibers are drawn or cut from gold, silver, copper, and aluminum and are made tarnish-proof by coating with plastic. Frequently the plastic is dyed, adding bright colors to the natural glitter of the metal. Metallic yarns come in many different forms—thin ribbons, wound around a core of linen or cotton, which strengthens and supports the thread, and other combinations. The handweaver must note whether the yarn is reinforced or not and should always weave brittle and breakable metallics together with another, stronger yarn.

SYNTHETIC FIBERS

Synthetic or man-made fibers are so widely used in commercial fabrics and so versatile that it is impossible to do them justice in a brief space. They are derived from basic materials such as wood pulp, cellulose, minerals, petroleum, salts, and coal, but each has a different chemical and physical composition and therefore special characteristics. Many are water- and fireproof and hypoallergenic; most are very elastic and resistant to moths and mildew. Most are washable, but some melt when touched with an iron that is too hot. All are strong and durable. Their greatest attraction for the handweaver is the intensity and brilliance of their color and the great variety of textures in which they are available.

Rayon

Rayon was the first synthetic to be developed, when chemists learned to treat plant cellulose and draw it into filaments. It was actually developed as a replacement and substitute for silk. There are several types of rayon, as well as several different registered trade names, each with individual properties.

Viscose rayon is very strong and is for this reason used in tire cords as well as textile fabrics. Another form is cuprammonium rayon. Each yarn reacts differently to dyes, and several kinds of rayon dyed with the same color can give interesting shades in woven fabrics.

Fortisan is a trade name for one of the strongest rayon fibers available; in it the molecules that form a strand are aligned parallel to the direction of the strand, giving it tremendous strength and resistance to stretching and shrinking. It is extremely fine and supple, and it can be used for very sheer fabrics such as curtains and gauzes.

2-17. Nylon: filament, staple, two-color blending, yarn, and woven fabric.

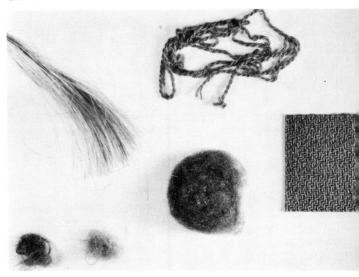

Acetate

Acetate is a fiber made from cellulose acetate; it can be made bright or dull, light or heavy, smooth or fuzzy, depending on the method of manufacture. It is resistant to moths, mildew, and mold, hypoallergenic, and a good insulator. Arnel and Celanese are familiar trade names of triacetate fibers.

Acrylic

Acrylic fibers are soft to the touch, have brilliant colors, can be made into wash-and-wear garments, and resist fading.

Polyester

Dacron is the most familiar trade name for polyester fiber, a synthetic with high tensile strength and resistance to abrasion. It blends well with other fibers such as wool and cotton and other synthetics.

Nylon

Nylon is the name for a group of synthetic products made from coal, petroleum, and natural gas. It is probably the most important man-made fiber and is used for a great variety of items. Nylon is mildew-proof, dries faster than any other textile, and needs little or no ironing. It has a very high tensile strength. When dry, it is stronger than silk, but it has a much lower absorbency. Because of its strength it is used for fishlines, tennis-racket strings, and parachutes; because of its elasticity, it is used for hosiery and lingerie. Spun nylon is produced by commercial spinners from nylon staple short length and spun into soft, fuzzy yarns. For the handweaver it is a good fiber to mix with natural yarns or to use by itself for strength and washability.

The yarn count of synthetic fibers is based on the same principles as the count of natural fibers. Synthetics spun like worsted are treated like natural worsted yarns; those spun like woolen yarn are treated like these yarns; and the fine filament synthetics are measured in deniers.

NOVELTY YARNS

A large variety of yarns, both natural and man-made, makes up the category of novelty, or specialty, yarns. These are spun and plied to produce nubs, twists, loops, and curls, and they are available under such names as bouclé, flake yarn, nub and seed yarn, ratiné, slub, and loop yarn.

FINISHING

The finishing processes used by handweavers for woven fabrics are very different from those used for commercially woven textiles. The latter are subjected to various specialized procedures, such as fulling (which compresses the fibers in newly woven fabric into a homogeneous whole), shrinking, pressing, sizing, bleaching, shearing, felting, napping, and texturizing; other procedures are used to make fabrics wrinkle resistant, water repellent, and fireproof.

In general, there are three main kinds of finish. The natural texture of the fibers may be left (e.g., keeping the fuzziness of woolens and tweeds). This is called natural finishing. The surface fibers in woven cloth may be sheared or singed so that the weave structure shows as clearly as when it came from the loom. This is called clear finishing. Finally, a nap may be brushed over the weave structure so that it is no longer visible. This is called face finishing.

Two final finishing processes are common to both commercial and handwoven fabrics—shrinking and pressing. The treatment depends on the individual material and the use for which it is intended. Some pieces, such as wall hangings, need no more than careful hemming by hand, fringing, and light steam pressing; other pieces, such as drapery or upholstery fabrics, require shrinking by steam pressing or dry cleaning by a professional cleaner (who can also apply stain- and water-repellent finishes).

Fabrics woven for wearing apparel demand the most careful attention, Silk, cotton, linen, and blends of fibers should be professionally finished. Although commercial cotton and linen wash excellently, the handweaver's work is often loosely woven and becomes limp, dull, and lifeless when washed. Unless a sample is tested and proves otherwise, these fabrics should be shrunk and pressed professionally.

Specialty yarns can be finished by brushing the fibers to create a surface nap. However, the fabrics should be professionally shrunk and cleaned, because they mat easily.

In general, wool fabrics can be finished by the weaver, although a sample should be tested. The procedure is to wash the fabric several times in lukewarm water with a mild detergent. It should be rinsed in water of the same temperature until the water remains clear. Then the fabric is squeezed (but not wrung) and hung by the selvage in the shade or rolled in towels to dry over night. A good steam pressing will give the fabric its final beauty.

3

THE WARP

The first step in the weaving of any fabric is to design the warp and warp the loom. Designing a warp for a sample piece is a good start for the beginner and a testing ground for the experienced weaver. For the beginner it provides an opportunity to explore the possibilities of yarns, colors, and textures and to observe the results of mixing them: his choices depend entirely on his imagination, adventurous spirit, and common sense. The experienced weaver-designer has the same opportunity, but he must also consider the specific requirements of his piece.

To make an experimental piece, these basic preliminary points must be decided: the kind of warp threads, the length of the warp, the number of warp threads (ends) to the inch, the width of the warp, and the total number of warp ends to be prepared.

A few simple rules have to be observed in choosing the warp threads. Any yarn—wool, cotton, silk, linen, synthetic, or blend—may be used if it is strong, relatively smooth, and nonabrasive. Very hairy and very nubby yarns should be avoided: save them for the weft. (If you *must* use a fuzzy yarn for the warp, select a coarse reed to reduce abrasion and strain, and double the threads in the dents wherever necessary.) Whether it is coarse or fine, smooth or textured, shiny or dull, any warp yarn must be able to withstand great tension when stretched on the loom.

All kinds of wool may be used, as long as the yarn has good tensile strength. Wool should never be stretched too tightly or left wound on spools, for it will lose its elasticity and become dead and hard.

Silk has good tensile strength, but the stronger, plied or spun silk yarns are better for the warp than fine, untwisted silk filaments. Cotton yarns may also be used, especially the strong and lustrous mercerized threads. Because linen is not elastic, it is more difficult to handle, and special attention must be paid to selecting strong, round yarns for the warp; single-ply or tow linen can only be used for weft.

An easy test for tensile strength is a quick pull of the yarn between the hands. If it breaks easily, it should not be chosen for the warp. In general, yarns that are not spun with a strong twist and single (unplied) yarns that come apart easily are not good warp yarns.

DESIGNING THE WARP

The simplest warp, of course, consists of the same yarn all across. Repeating sequences of different warp threads can be worked out in any number, from alternating threads to a long repeat pattern. It is also possible to make a warp that does not repeat at all across the width of the loom. In mixing yarns, however, remember that using very coarse and very fine threads in the same warp influences the overall tension of the warp. A combination of the two will work when the yarns are in alternating sequence—one thick, one thin—but not when groups of each kind are alternated. The thin threads will wind tightly on the warp beam, while the heavy threads pile up, so the even tension necessary for good weaving cannot be maintained. This problem can only be avoided by using two warp beams, one for the thin and another for the heavy threads.

To get acquainted with some of the possibilities of warping, try the following project. You will need some

3-1. Yarns of various textures arranged in a possible warp sequence.

3-2. Yarns arranged in a possible warp sequence.

The spacing of the warp threads in the reed depends on the kind of fabric to be woven: there are three design alternatives. The warp in the woven fabric may have the same prominence as the weft; the weft may hide the warp completely (this is called weft-faced material); or the warp may hide the weft completely (a warp-faced material). The size of the yarn must also be taken into account: if the yarn is fine, a higher number of threads per inch is required; if it is coarse, fewer threads are needed. If the warp is meant to cover the weft, the threads have to be set very closely together in the reed—they may be doubled or tripled in the dents. (Threading through the reed is called sleying; single, double, or triple sleying means that one, two, or three threads are drawn through a dent.) If a weft-faced material is planned, fewer warp threads are needed, and dents may be skipped.

Thus, the number of warp threads per inch is not determined by the reed, because the threads may be doubled, tripled, or skipped. The deciding factor is the desired texture of the fabric, which in turn depends on its design, weight, and function.

For fabric in which warp and weft are to have equal prominence, these guidelines may be followed: a homespun or tweed yarn for suiting will usually work well within the range of fifteen to twenty-four threads per inch. Drapery or upholstery fabrics will be satisfactory with a setting of fifteen to eighteen threads per inch for the weight of a number 5 pearl cotton. For tapestries and rugs, a linen or cotton number 10/5 yarn may be set at five to eight threads per inch.

Many variations are possible, of course, and the warping will finally be determined by all of the factors discussed here. Making a sample will help with the final decision.

WARPING THE LOOM

There are many different methods of warping the loom. Every weaver develops a preference for one or another and will insist that his is the best and easiest. I will describe two methods that I find useful—chain warping and sectional warping. (Instructions for calculating the total yardage of yarn needed for warping are given in an appendix.)

Chain Warping

In chain warping, all the warp threads used across the entire width of the loom are measured at the same time and wound on the warp beam at the same time. This process is most efficient when short warps (five yards or less) or narrow warps are being prepared. Some advantages of the method are that warping can be done with a single spool for each color and the warp sequence can be designed without a repeat. On the other hand, all the warp threads are handled at the same time; therefore, great care is needed to keep them in order and untangled. Two people are needed—one to

cardboard, masking tape, and scissors, as well as a variety of yarns. Out of the cardboard, cut nine 3- by 5-inch rectangles. Lengthwise around each piece of cardboard wind a warp sequence based on these suggestions: (1) three warp sequences of yarns that have the same texture but different colors; (2) three sequences with different textures but the same color; (3) three sequences with different colors and different textures. As you wind, fasten the threads on the back of the cardboard with bits of masking tape.

These experiments will produce nine different warps. One or more of them can be used for a sample on the loom, and they can all be mounted together on a large matboard and used for reference and decoration.

When a warp is designed for a particular project, the ultimate use of the fabric must be considered carefully. A warp for clothing fabric should be soft, flexible, and not bulky. A warp for upholstery fabric must be especially strong, with no weak points in any of the threads, and able to withstand a great amount of stretching and abrasion. Drapery material must have a warp that will hang straight, be flexible enough to allow draping, and strong enough to support the weft without sagging under its weight.

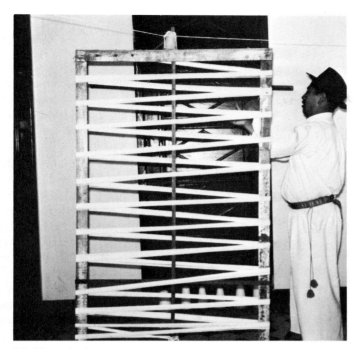

3-3. Weaver in Quito, Ecuador, preparing warp on a warping tree.

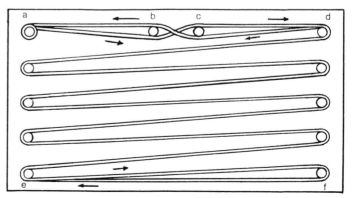

3-4. Student winding three-yard warp on a small warping board.

wind the warp on the beam, the other to hold all the threads in tension. A warping board or tree is also necessary.

The following procedure is simple and efficient for putting up chain warps. It does not matter whether the beam is plain or sectional.

(1) Determine the number of warp ends needed. Multiply the desired width of the material by the number of warp ends you plan to use per inch, and add two threads to each side for selvages. For example, if you want a fabric to be ten inches wide and you are using fifteen threads per inch, the total number of warp ends necessary is 10 times 15, or 150, plus 4 selvage threads; you will have to wind 154 threads for your warp.

(2) Determine the length of the warp. (A good length for a sample piece is three to five yards.) For a specific project, add thirty-six inches to the length of the piece for tying and waste. If you plan to weave more than one piece on the same warp, the length of the warp must equal the sum of all lengths plus the length for tying and waste plus about six inches between pieces. Additional length must be allowed for fringes or hems. For example, if you want to make a forty-inch-long fringed scarf, you will need 40 inches plus 36 inches for tying and waste plus 10 inches for fringe, making a total length of 86 inches. For two scarves of the same length, add another 40 inches plus 10 inches for fringe plus 6 inches between, making a total of 142 inches.

(3) Wind the warp on a warping board or tree. If you are using a skein, place it on a skein winder. If you are using spools, place them on a spool rack; if you are winding from several spools at a time, arrange them on the rack so that they all unwind in the same direction.

As illustrated in Figure 3-5, tie the end of the first thread to the first peg (a) on the board. Carry the thread under peg b and over peg c to peg d and on to other pegs according to the length desired. (The standard distance between pegs on a warping board is one yard,

3-5. Measuring a five-yard warp on a warping board (a) and a ten-yard warp measured on the same warping board (b).

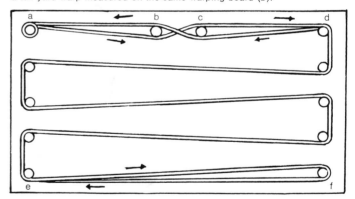

(a)

(b)

and the length of each side of a warping tree is also a yard.) At the last peg (peg *f* in the illustration), start the thread on the return trip. When it returns to pegs *b* and *c*, it travels under *c* and over *b*. These are therefore called the cross, or lease, pegs. The crisscrossing of the warp thread at the lease pegs is very important, because it keeps them in order for the process of entering (threading them through the reed). With the return of the thread to peg *a*, the first and second warp threads have been measured. Note that color changes in the warp can only be made at the beginning or end (*a* and *f* in the example given).

(4) Count threads. Count at the lease in groups of ten as you wind. Loop a thread of a different color over the counted groups as a marker so you do not have to recount.

(5) Remove threads from the warping board or tree. First, secure the lease by putting a piece of string and then two rods (or empty heddles) through each part of the crossed threads and taping these lease rods to each other with masking tape on each end. Leave a distance of about two inches between the rods (see Figure 3-8). Tie a piece of colored string tightly around all the warp threads near peg *b*, another near peg *c*, and another near the end part of the warp at *f*. You can also tie the warp threads between each two pegs. (On a warping tree, tie the threads near the pegs at the beginning and end and on several sections in between.) Now cut the warp at *f*, which is the end of the warp chain and the farthest point from the lease.

(6) Make a chain as illustrated in Figure 3-9 by making a loop of the warp with the cut end and slipping your right hand through it, grasping the warp threads above the loop, and pulling them through to make a new loop. Continue this procedure in crochet-stitch fashion until the warp is off the board and chained up to the two lease rods.

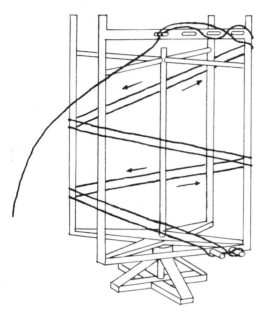

3-6. Winding a four-yard warp on a warping tree.

3-7. Crossing the warp threads to make the cross or lease.

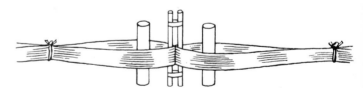

3-8. Securing the cross at the lease pegs.

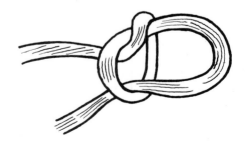

3-9. Starting to make a warp chain. Grasp the warp threads and pull them through the loop.

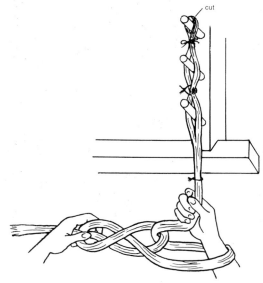

3-10. The warp chain before it is removed from the warping board.

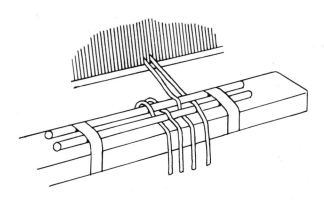

3-11. Sleying—entering the warp threads in the dents.

(7) Sley (enter the warp in the reed) as follows. Place the warp chain on a chair in front of the breast beam, with the lease rods resting on the beam. Tie or tape the rods to the beam securely. Carefully cut the end of the warp chain at the end taken off peg *a*. Pull the warp ends toward the beater to prevent them from slipping away from the lease rods. Locate the center of the reed and measure one-half the width of the piece on one side. (The warp should be centered on the loom.) Have ready a threading hook and with it enter each thread through the reed, alternating threads coming over and under the lease. Tie in groups behind the reed as you thread to prevent the ends from pulling back through the reed. Put two threads in each of the outside dents for selvages. (The selvage threads are double in the reed, single in the heddles.)

(8) Thread the ends through the eyes in the heddles according to the weave pattern (Figures 3-12 and 3-13). Tie in groups with an overhand knot (Figures 3-14 and 3-15) to prevent the threads from slipping back through the heddles. Check the threading as you go along.

3-12. Threading the warp threads through the heddles.

3-13. View from the back of the loom of the threads threaded through the heddles.

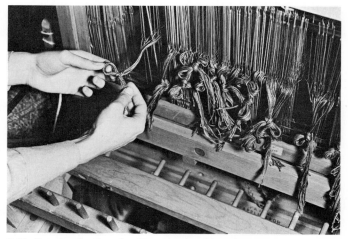

3-14. Securing the threads with an overhand loop knot.

3-15. Overhand knot. This knot can be easily opened by pulling one end.

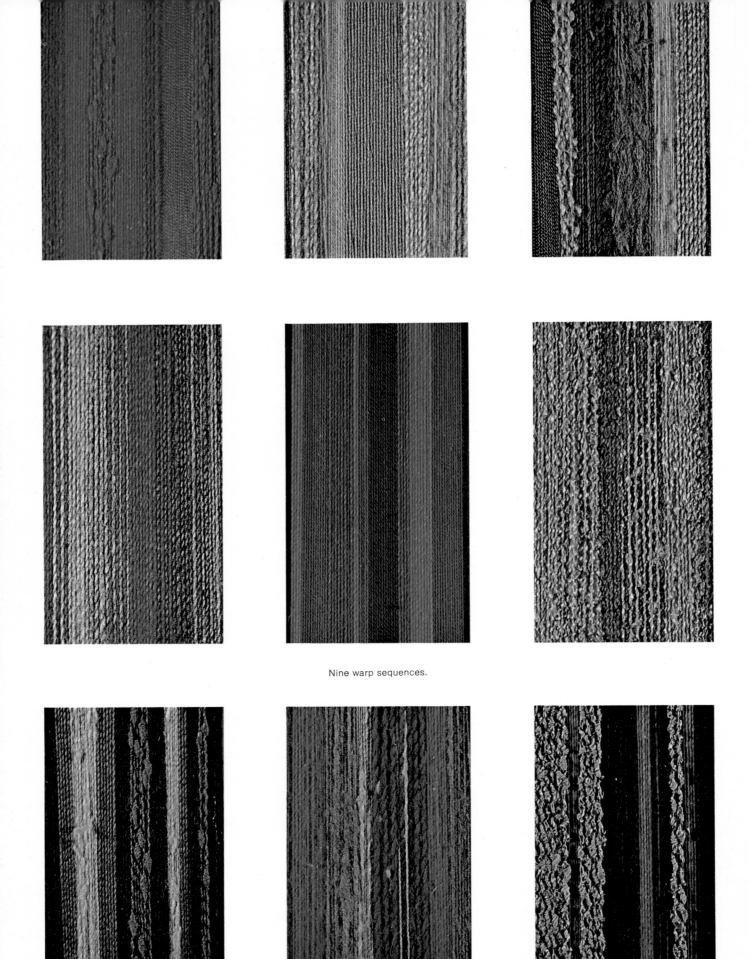

Nine warp sequences.

(9) Group the ends of the threads and tie them to the apron rod at the back of the loom with a square knot (Figure 3-16). Make sure that the threads come straight from the reed toward the beam. Before taking the next step, check the threading again to verify each heddle and each dent.

(10) Beaming. Straighten out the threads and heddles so that each thread is in its place at right angles to the beater and the warp beam. Before winding the warp on the warp beam, comb out tangles with your fingers or a brush; comb about four feet of warp at a time. To ensure even tension, one person should hold the threads taut in front of the loom while another winds threads on the back beam. Place a flat stick into the warp parallel to the beam at intervals. This will prevent uneven tension and keep the winding smooth. Insert newspapers in the same way to prevent warp threads from piling unevenly. (If the warp beam is sectional, the stick and newspapers will not be necessary.) Wind the entire warp, leaving about half a yard hanging in front of the beater. Trim warp ends so that they are all the same length.

(11) Gating. Tie small bunches (groups of about eight threads) to the apron rod in front of the loom. First tie them with a single knot, then check the tension and tie securely into bows (Figure 3-18). Be sure the groups are evenly distributed and at right angles to the beater.

(12) On a foot loom, tie each lam to a treadle with an adjustable snitch (slip) knot (Figure 3-20), or tie up according to the weave pattern. Treadle to raise alternate threads. Weave in some heavy yarn until the warp threads are spread evenly and a firm heading (beginning) has been made.

If the shed is not good, check to see that the loom is properly adjusted. Harnesses must be even. On a foot loom, lams must be horizontal and even, and treadles should hang evenly about four inches from the

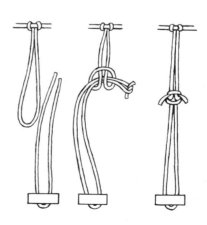

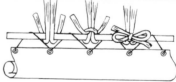

3-18, 3-19. Tying the warp threads to the front apron rod and the three steps in making the knot.

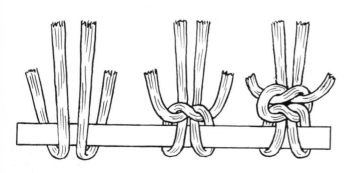

3-16. Tying the warp threads in a square knot on the back apron rod (three steps).

3-20. Tying the lams to the treadles with adjustable snitch knots (three steps).

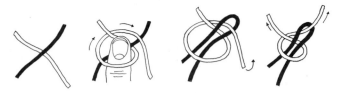

3-21. Weaver's knot.

floor. These adjustments should be made at the start.

If, when you are finished weaving, you wish to avoid the entering part of the preparation for a new project, you can use the warp that remains on the loom. Tie up the threads in knots or tape them to prevent slipping. Make a new warp chain with the same number of threads. Tie the lease rods and warp to the breast beam at the front of the loom. Tie each new thread to the corresponding old thread with a weaver's knot (Figure 3-21) and pull threads carefully through the reed and heddles. Then continue with beaming and gating.

Sectional Warping

In sectional warping, the warp, in sections, goes directly from spools through a tensioner on to the warp beam. This method is most efficient for long and wide warps with a repeat of no more than two inches (most sectional warp beams have pegs spaced at two-inch intervals). Because the warp is wound directly on the warp beam and not handled at all, it can be kept in order very easily. Also, one person can wind the warp on the beam very quickly. Another advantage is that the tension of the warp is the same for each section. However, it is necessary to wind as many spools of yarn as are needed for one two-inch section. Instead of winding the whole warp in a chain, one section is rolled on at a time; then the warp is cut, the spool rack and tensioner are moved, and the next section is rolled on the same way. The procedure is as follows:

(1) Determine the number of warp ends needed for two inches. For example, if you plan to use fifteen threads to the inch, you will have thirty threads on two inches. You will therefore need thirty spools plus two extra spools on the outside sections for the selvages.

(2) Wind enough yarn on each spool to fill each section across the width of the loom.

(3) Put the filled spools on the spool rack starting on the upper right side and going down in the sequence of your color scheme. Start again at the top and fill the spool rack in the same way until all the spools are on in the right sequence (see Figure 3-22). Be sure that each beginning thread comes from the top of the spool.

(4) Fasten the warp tensioner on the back beam directly over the section to be wound. The best way to start is from the middle of the warp beam and fill each section on each side as the warping proceeds. This keeps the warp in the center of the loom if you should run out of thread prematurely (this should not happen, but sometimes it does!).

(5) Guide each warp thread from the spool in its right order through the tensioner. Some tensioners have a reed or a piece with holes at the end through which each warp thread has to be guided (see Figure 3-22). (If you are using a different kind of tensioner, follow the directions of the manufacturer.) Make sure that you use as many holes or spaces as will spread the warp evenly for the two inches. Then each warp thread goes over and under the wooden pegs of the tensioner.

(6) When all the threads are in the tensioner, tie the collected ends to the stick on the warp beam in the center of the section (Figure 3-23).

(7) Turn the warp beam—slowly at first—and be sure to turn in the right direction, so that the warp will unwind correctly in weaving. Check to see that the section of warp runs directly between the pegs. If it does not, it is probably because the tensioner is not exactly centered; just push it one way or the other a little.

On most looms, each turn of the warp beam puts a yard on the beam; on others, it may be necessary to make two or more turns to the yard. Count the number of turns you put on carefully. If you mark one of the pegs on your starting turn, it will be easy to know when one turn has been completed. Keep a pencil and paper handy to jot down the number immediately if you have to stop. If you are in doubt about how many turns you have put on, it is better to have an extra turn on a sec-

3-22. The warp threads traveling from the spool rack through the tensioner to the loom.

3-23. Side view of warp threads in tensioner.

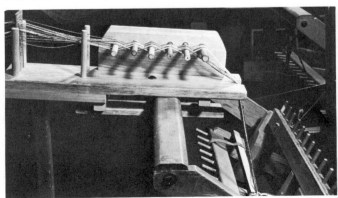

3-24. The warp threads being threaded through the heddles.

3-25. The warp threads being threaded through the reed.

tion than one too few, which could mean spoiling the rest of the piece.

(8) When the proper number of turns, or yards, has been put on a section, use a piece of masking tape to secure the ends until you are ready to thread them through the heddles. Cut a strip of tape twice as wide as the section, slide it under the taut threads about three or four inches below the tensioner, and fold it over to hold the threads in place. Roll on about six or eight inches more and tape the ends to the wound threads with another piece of tape. Cut off, and move the tensioner to the next section. Repeat the process until the width of the loom is filled.

If a spool runs out of thread before the warping is finished, replace the empty spool with a full one, taking care to keep the threads in the right order. Always try to replace the spools at the beginning of a section to avoid having knots in the warp: tie the end of the new thread to the old one with a weaver's knot (see Figure 3-21), pull the knot through the tensioner, and clip it off.

(9) Drawing in the heddles and sleying. Count the heddles on each harness to be sure you have the right number. When the whole warp beam is filled, take one section of threads at a time and fasten the ends to the back beam with masking tape. Repeat until all sections of warp are securely taped to the back beam. Then unroll the warp beam little by little, until the warp ends are just long enough to reach the reed in front of the loom. Thread one section at a time through the heddles. Draw each thread through the eye of one heddle, according to your pattern. Continue until the whole warp is drawn into the heddles (Figure 3-24). Tie in small bunches with an overhand knot. Then thread the warp through the reed (Figure 3-25).

(10) Tie the warp in small bunches to the apron rod in front of the loom, as in chain warping. Tighten and check the tension so that it is even all across the warp. Tie the treadles according to the weave pattern. Then start weaving with heavy yarn until the warp threads are spread evenly and a firm heading has been made.

When the loom has been warped, weaving can begin. The process is composed of three basic steps, which are then repeated. These steps are:

3-26. The weaving has started.

(1) Depress treadle according to the design to open shed. Move beater towards you and then back against the loom frame. This clears the shed.

(2) Throw (slide) the shuttle with the weft through the shed. This is called a pick or shot. Leave the beginning end of weft hanging out about an inch.

(3) Press (beat) the weft towards you with the beater and move the beater back. This completes the first cycle of weaving.

(4) Depress the next treadle. Move the beater towards you again and then back against the frame to clear the shed.

(5) Throw shuttle from the opposite side through the shed and fold the loose end of weft yarn into the same shed (this need only be done the first time).

(6) Beat the weft into place and repeat from the start. Be careful not to pull in the edges. Weaving is a rhythmical process: smooth motions and speed will soon be acquired by practice.

4

EXPLORING THE WEAVES

Weaves are formed by the interlacing of warp and weft threads passed over and under each other. The structure of the fabric is determined by the way this interlacing occurs. Knowing the basic weave constructions intimately is a solid foundation for the beginner and a stepping-stone for the experienced weaver. Basic weaves become as familiar to the weaver as daily bread and are indeed the primary fare of the weavers craft. They can be used in so many variations and with so many fresh and imaginative seasonings that they certainly never need be dull.

There are literally thousands of weave constructions to explore. Many excellent books, some of which are listed in the Bibliography, discuss a multitude of weaves and provide a never-ending field for discovery. It is not possible to give an exhaustive coverage of all weaves and techniques in one book. My intention is to discuss basic constructions and methods that I find most stimulating and rewarding. The better the weaver understands these fundamentals, the freer he is to adapt them creatively to his own ideas and purposes.

THE BASIC WEAVES

Plain Weave

Plain weave, which is called tabby in the weaver's language, is the simplest and most important of all weave structures. In it, each warp interlaces with each weft in an alternating fashion, making the weave very strong and the material somewhat stiff. Plain weave is used in about 80 percent of all commercial fabrics, and is also the foundation for many other techniques. It can be

woven on any number of harnesses, but since its construction is based on alternating warp threads being raised and lowered, it is the foremost pattern used on the two-harness loom.

Twill

Twill is a versatile basic weave that possesses nearly unlimited possibilities for variation. The structure of twills is based on the overlapping and staggering of warp and weft threads, which produces diagonal lines in the material. Twill lines may run from left to right (right-hand twill) or from right to left (left-hand twill). Usually, twill lines woven on four harnesses have an angle of 45 degrees, but other diagonals can be worked out.

Satin Weave

Weave constructions similar to irregular twills are found in a group of weaves called satin weaves. They are used mostly as a basis for damask and brocaded fabrics. The points where warps and wefts interlock are arranged so that diagonal lines are avoided, in order to make smooth and sometimes shiny surfaces. Because this distribution results in loosely interlocked constructions which need extremely fine and close settings of the warp, these weaves are rarely satisfactory for the handweaver and are not discussed here.

DRAFTING

Drafting weaves may seem a puzzling and laborious task to the beginner, but it provides the key to an enormous range of understanding. It is the guide for exploring weaves beyond a teacher's instruction, and it enables the weaver to design patterns at will. Throughout this book I use a method of drafting that I have found both easy and useful. It is based on the action of the rising shed or jack-type loom. A simple way to transform the directions for use with a sinking shed or counter-balanced loom will be found in an appendix.

The complete draft gives a picture of the four essential factors in weaving: the threading of the warp through the heddles, the tie-up (the combination of harnesses to be raised), the sequence of treadling, and the weave or pattern.

In threading, the warp threads are drawn through the heddles in a predetermined sequence. Changes in the threading sequence change the resulting pattern. The simplest threading is the straight threading (often called twill threading): on a four-harness loom, the first warp thread is drawn through the first heddle of the first harness, the second warp thread through the first heddle of the second harness, the third warp thread through the first heddle of the third harness, and the fourth warp thread through the first heddle of the fourth harness. This is repeated across the width of the loom until all warp threads are drawn through the heddles in the right order. For eight harnesses the same sequence is followed, continuing through the eighth harness.

The tie-up determines how the harnesses are raised. They may be raised one at a time or in combination; on a table loom these combinations are made by pressing the levers by hand, while on a foot loom the combinations are tied on through the lams to the foot treadles.

A standard plain weave tie-up is:
> harnesses 1 and 3 tied to treadle 1
> harnesses 2 and 4 tied to treadle 2

A standard twill tie-up is:
> harnesses 1 and 2 tied to treadle 1
> harnesses 2 and 3 tied to treadle 2
> harnesses 3 and 4 tied to treadle 3
> harnesses 4 and 1 tied to treadle 4

The sequence in which the tie-up combinations are used is called the treadling. Any change in the treadling sequence makes a change in the pattern.

In this book, the threading sequence is designated by numbers separated by comas, e.g., 1,2,3,4; the tie-up of the harnesses, by numbers separated by hyphens, e.g., 1-2-3-4.

The symbols for drafting vary in different publications, but the principle of drafts is the same no matter how they are written. Since weavers are frequently confused by the variations, a list of different symbols used is given in an appendix.

Drafting of threadings, tie-ups, treadlings, and patterns can be worked out on graph paper. *Note that the drafts are read from the bottom up.* Graph paper that is divided into eight squares to the inch, with inch-squares indicated by heavier lines, is recommended. Each square represents a heddle on a harness. Each number in a square represents a warp thread in that heddle.

Drafting the Threading

The straight (twill) threading on a four-harness loom is drafted this way:

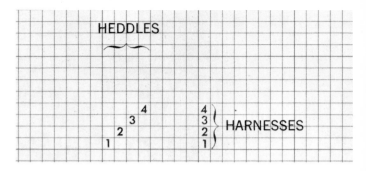

Drafting the Tie-Up

The tie-up is represented by dots parallel to the threading. Thus, the tie-up for a plain weave with the straight threading is drafted this way:

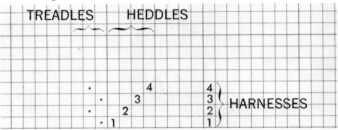

and for a standard twill, this way:

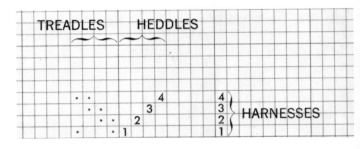

Drafting the Treadling

The treadling sequence is represented by vertical lines below the tie-up dots. To use the examples just given, the plain weave treadling is drafted this way:

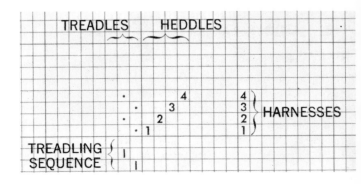

and the standard twill, this way:

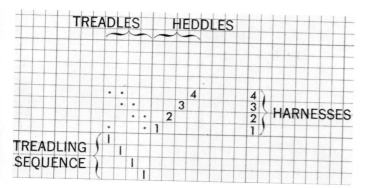

Drafting the Pattern

The pattern results from the combination of tie-up and treadling sequence and is represented by filled and unfilled squares. Each filled square represents a warp thread being lifted. *The draft of the pattern must correspond to the draft of the threading.*

The complete draft for the plain weave example given above looks like this:

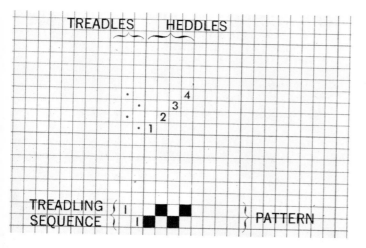

while the twill looks like this:

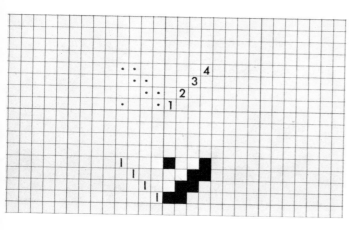

The same system applies for the drafting of two-harness and eight-harness weaves. A plain-weave draft for two harnesses is:

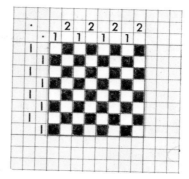

and for eight harnesses:

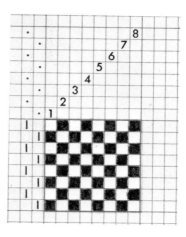

In drafting, one repeat of the pattern usually suffices to indicate the weave. For some patterns, however, several repeats are necessary to show the weave's true appearance.

When warp or weft color is important for a pattern, the colors are indicated in the draft, supplanting the numbers in the threading and the vertical lines in the treadling. Figure 4-34, among others, illustrates the color draft.

THE WEAVER'S RECORDS

It is indispensable for a weaver to keep correct records of important pieces he has woven so that they can be reproduced at a later time. The records may be kept in a notebook, folders, or any other system of filing information. It is good practice to write down new combinations as made in the course of weaving, or immediately afterwards. The record should contain the following: the warp sequence, the weft sequence, the setting in the reed, the complete draft with threading, tie-up (including color changes), treadling, and pattern. Samples of warp and weft yarns used and a swatch of the woven material or a complete sample piece should also be kept.

4-1. Plain weave variations.
Draft for Fig. 4-1

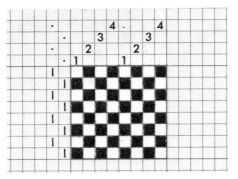

An experienced weaver will rarely undertake an important project without first making a sample. The quality of the yarns, the density of the warp, the colors, the threading and treadling of the design, and finally, the reaction of the fibers to washing, pressing, or dry-cleaning can only be tested by weaving a swatch.

It is much easier to record the pertinent information at the time the material is woven than to analyze it later, and the keeping of good records is an aspect of weaving that adds to the feeling of accomplishment which makes weaving such an enjoyable craft.

DERIVATIONS FROM THE BASIC WEAVES

Basket Weaves

Basket weaves are enlarged forms of plain weave, since they work on the system of alternating groups of threads being raised and lowered. In basket weave, two or more adjacent threads are lifted together and two or more weft threads are inserted together to make the weave square. Irregular basket weaves are produced by lifting and weaving irregular numbers of threads.

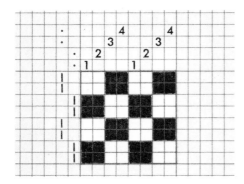

4-2. Basket weave.
Draft for Fig. 4-2

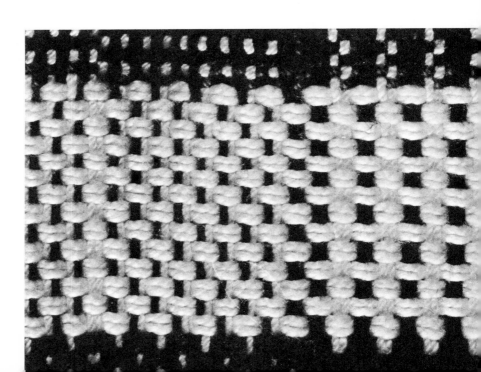

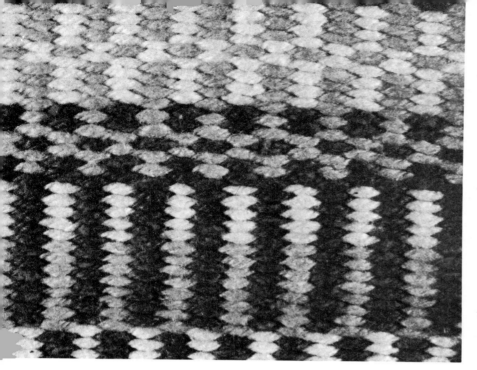

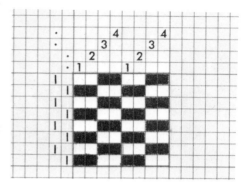

4-3. Basket weave variations.
Draft for Fig. 4-3.

Rib Weaves

Rib, or rep, weaves are also derived from plain weave. Two steps follow each other in regular repeat and build up a vertical pattern—for example, harnesses 2-3-4 up, harness 1 down; harness 1 up, harnesses 2-3-4 down. Other rib weaves are produced by alternating heavy and fine yarns in warp or weft. Closely set heavy and fine yarns alternating in the warp will make warp ribs (vertical ridges); if the yarns are alternated in the weft, weft ribs (horizontal ridges) will be formed.

Below:
4-4. Four-thread basket weave for two harnesses.

Right:
4-5. Four-thread basket weave for eight harnesses.

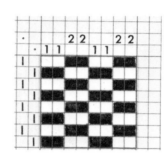

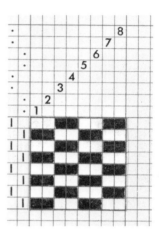

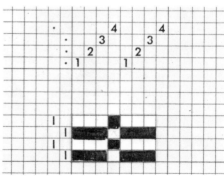

4-6. Rib weave.
Draft for Fig. 4-6.

4-7. A ²⁄₂ twill.

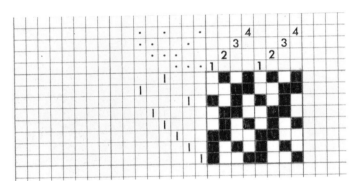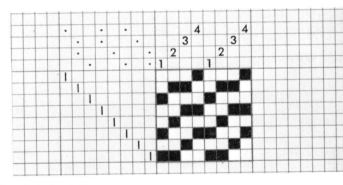

4-8. Steep twill (left) and slanting twill.

Four-Harness Twills

Twills may be balanced or unbalanced. Balanced twills show the same amount of warp and weft on each side of the fabric, while unbalanced twills have more warp than weft on one side and the opposite on the reverse side.

Twills are identified by numbers and slashes in the draft. For example, ²⁄₂ / stands for the standard twill (which is a balanced twill) of two warps up and two down. The top number indicates the warp threads that are raised, and the bottom number indicates the warp threads that stay down and are covered by the weft. The slash is the symbol for twill.

The balanced ²⁄₂ twill on a straight threading (Figure 4-9) is treadled:

1-2
2-3
3-4
4-1

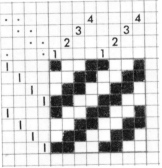

4-9. A ²⁄₂ twill for four harnesses.

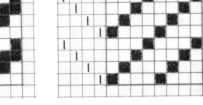

4-10. A ⅓ straight twill.

The unbalanced ⅓ twill (Figure 4-10) is treadled:

1
2
3
4

This produces a weft-faced construction—the weft covers the three warp threads that stay down. The reverse side is, therefore, warp-faced. To weave the same material with the warp-faced side up (which is a ³⁄₁ twill, Figure 4-11), the treadling is:

1-2-3
2-3-4
1-3-4
1-2-4

When the straight diagonal lines of a twill are interrupted and rearranged by treadling a different sequence, a broken twill is produced. For a ²⁄₂ broken twill (Figure 4-12) the treadling is:

1-2
2-3
1-4
3-4

For a ¹⁄₃ broken twill (Figure 4-13) treadling is:

1
2
4
3

And for a ³⁄₁ broken twill (Figure 4-14) the treadling is:

1-2-3
2-3-4
1-2-4
1-3-4

Many variations can be obtained by combining twills with each other or with plain weaves. The possibilities should be explored by inventing combinations directly on the loom.

Twills can also be varied by changing the direction of the twill lines during the course of weaving. Treadling

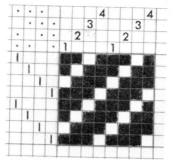

4-11. A ³⁄₁ straight twill.

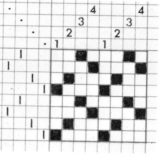

4-12. A ²⁄₂ broken twill.

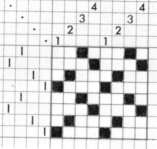

4-13. A ¹⁄₃ broken twill.   4-14. A ³⁄₁ broken twill.

4-15. Basket weave and twill combined.

4-16. Straight and broken twill combined.

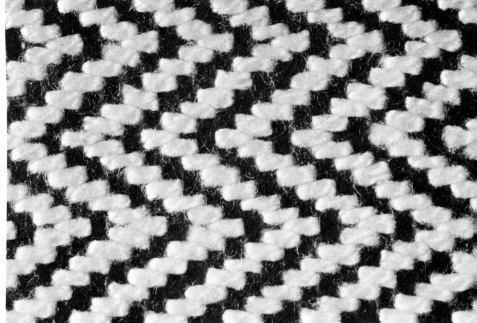

4-17. A ⅔ reversed twill.

Draft for Fig. 4-17

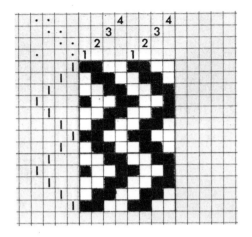

4-18. Plain weave and ⅓ reversed twill combined.

4-19. Herringbone or point twill.

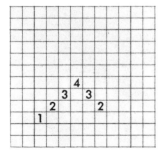

first in one direction and then in the other creates interesting reverse designs, such as that shown in Figure 4-17; treadling forward and backward in an irregular manner results in a pattern that looks like a bolt of lightning and is appropriately named "lightning twill" (see Figure 4-48).

Still other twills can be made by changes in threading. Among the arrangements possible is the point, or herringbone, threading (Figure 4-19). This transforms

4-20. Twill variations with herringbone threading, combining ⅓ and ³⁄₁ twills in the weaving.

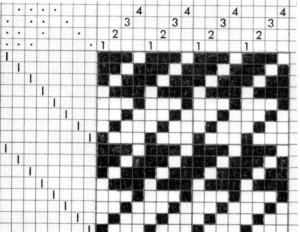

4-21. A ⅓ ³⁄₁ twill combined by treadling.

4-22. Herringbone variation woven on a black and white warp.

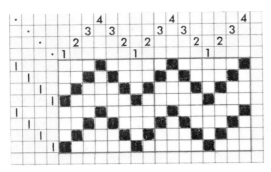

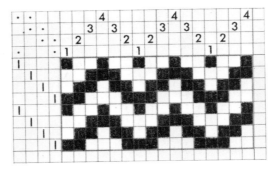

4-23. A ⅓ twill with a point twill threading (left) and a ²⁄₂ twill with a point twill threading.

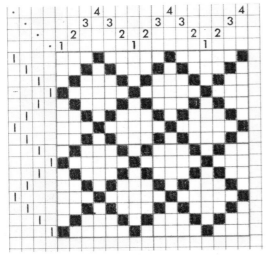

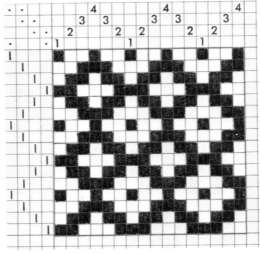

4-24. A point twill threading woven in ⅓ reversed twill, resulting in a diamond.

4-25. The same threading as in Fig. 4-24 woven in ²⁄₂ reversed twill.

the straight twill lines into a herringbone and the reversed twill into a diamond. Figures 4-23 through 4-25 show some of the many fascinating weaves different threadings can produce, even though tie-up and treadling may remain the same.

Another variation produced by the threading arrangement is the undulating twill. Warp threads can be doubled, tripled, or skipped in the heddles to produce wavy lines. The example shown in Figure 4-26 is threaded:

1,2,3,4
2,3,4
1,3,4
1
2,2
3,3,3
4,4

This results in a very textured-looking material.

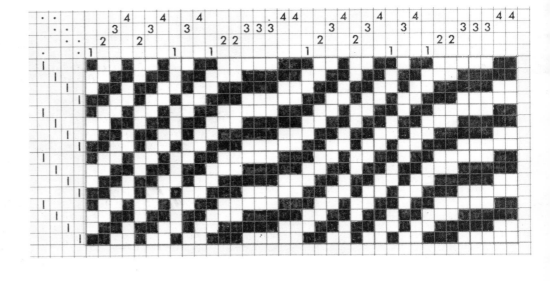

4-26. Undulating twill threading woven in ²⁄₂ twill.

COLOR PATTERNS (FOUR HARNESSES)

Arrangements of different colors in warp and weft will yield new and often surprising results in the same weaves. The weave construction itself moves into the background, and the colors create the design.

Stripes

Stripes are, of course, most prominent when they contrast with the background. Horizontal stripes are woven with weft yarns, and their color and texture can therefore be varied spontaneously. Vertical stripes must be planned in the warp.

4-27. Horizontal stripes in a wall hanging by R. V. Reitzenstein. Rickrack was incorporated into the design.

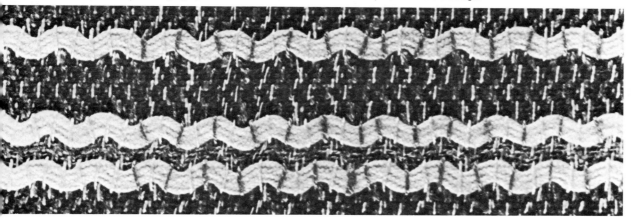

4-28. Horizontal stripes in drapery fabric by a student.

4-29. Vertical stripes in a wool shawl from Guatemala.

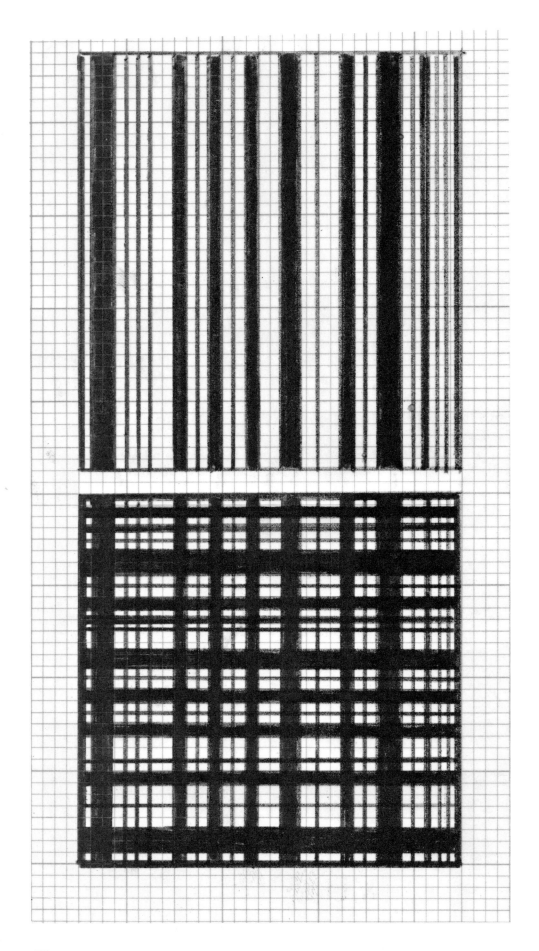

4-30. Warp and weft patterns for a plaid designed by Jay Hinz.

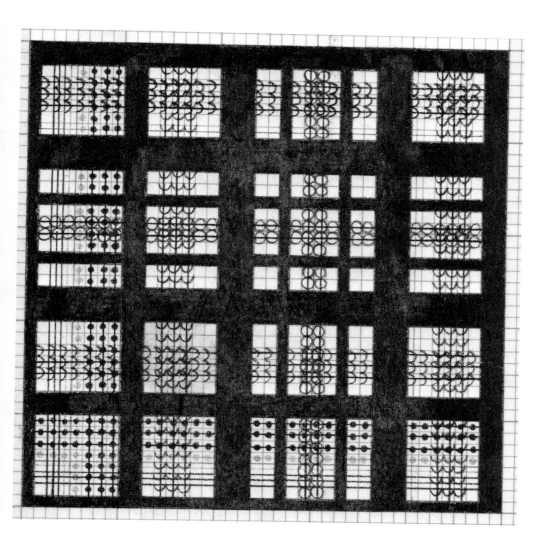

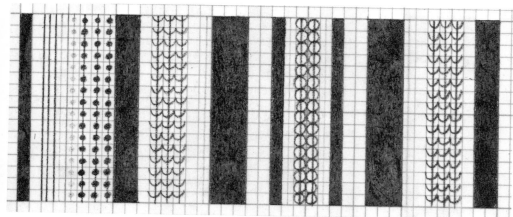

4-31. Plaid using various textures in warp and weft, designed by Jay Hinz.

Plaids

When warp and weft are composed of patterns of stripes, the result is a plaid material. Scottish tartans are based on repeats of colors in weft and warp. Designing plaids is a fascinating and rewarding project. Any number of colors can be combined in the stripes, and the

4-32. Plaid fabric in plain weave.

warp colors can be repeated in the weft in their exact sequence, or varied to please the weaver. Experiments in plain weaves, basket weaves, and twills should be made to explore the many possibilities for color and texture variation.

Checks

The difference between a plaid and a check is the size and regularity of the stripes. While a plaid material has wide bands of many different colors, the check is usually formed by small units of regularly arranged light and dark yarns. These units usually range from two to sixteen threads. A tiny shepherd's check is woven alternating two dark and two light threads in warp and weft in plain weave (Figure 4-33). When woven with four dark and four light threads in plain weave, the result is a different check (Figure 4-34). These designs are formed by the way the light and dark threads cross. When a dark warp thread is raised, it covers the weft under it, and therefore produces a dark color on the surface. When a light thread is raised, it produces a light color, even if the weft under it is dark.

4-33. Shepherd's check in plain weave.

Right:
4-34. Large check in plain weave.

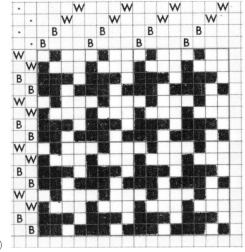
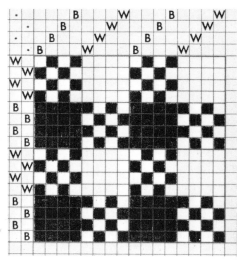

(B=black, W=white)

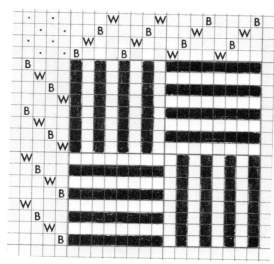

4-35. Log-cabin pattern in plain weave.

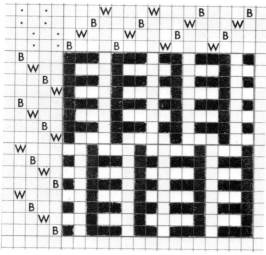

4-36. Log-cabin pattern shown in Fig. 4-35 in basket weave.

4-37. Log-cabin variations made by color changes in the warp.

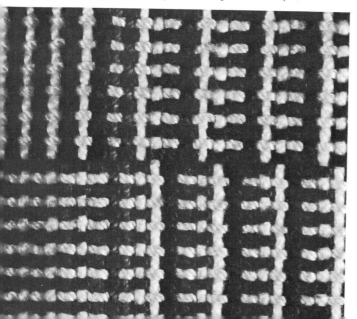

Log-Cabin Pattern

The log-cabin pattern is best described by its name. Blocks of horizontal and vertical pinstripes form the logs (Figure 4-35). Since the pattern has a plain-weave construction, it can be made on a two-harness loom. Light and dark colors alternate in warp and weft. One light thread and one dark thread are put alternately through the heddles for the width of one block. At the point of change, the colors are switched, or thrown over to opposite harnesses. This is done by placing two light or dark threads next to each other and then resuming the threading of alternate dark and light. In the warp the switching points have to be determined before the pattern is threaded; in the weft the change can be made spontaneously.

The size and proportion of the logs can be varied by changing the placement of the switching points in the warp and weft; a dark or a light thread in the warp or weft may be replaced by a third color at the switching points, making an overplaid. The texture of the yarns may also be varied. The log-cabin threading sequence may be used to make a basket-weave pattern in light and dark variations (Figure 4-38), and a step pattern may be achieved by weaving the same in a ⅔ twill treadling (Figure 4-39).

4-38. Fabric woven in a combination of plain weave and basket weave.

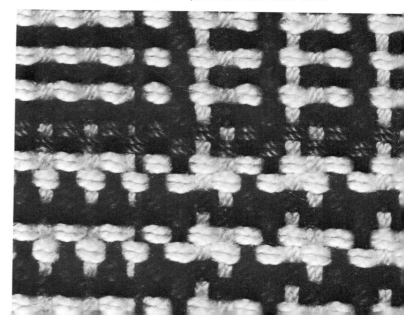

4-39. A step pattern made by weaving one dark thread, one light thread in a 2/2 twill.
Draft for Fig. 4-39.

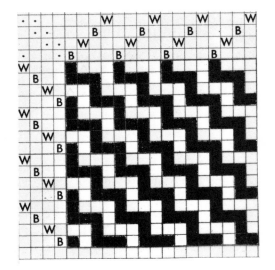

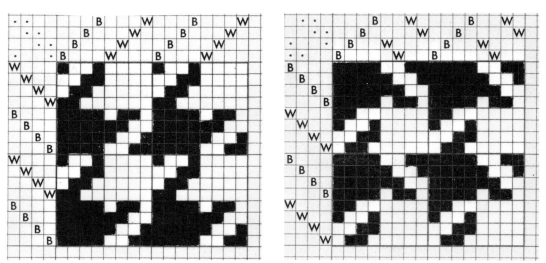

4-40. Houndstooth with straight threading (left) and with rearranged order of threading.

Houndstooth Patterns

Houndstooth patterns are based on checks of four dark and four light threads in the warp and weft. As Figure 4-40 illustrates, a straight threading woven in ⅔ twill results in an irregular and not particularly attractive houndstooth; for a clearer, more defined outline, the threading sequence must be changed:

1,2,3,4—dark
2,1,4,3—light

There are many variations of the color patterns. Several combinations can be put on the loom at the same time, yielding such interesting patterns as those in Figures 4-41 through 4-44.

4-41. Threading variation in upholstery fabric designed by Helen Little.
Draft for Fig. 4-41

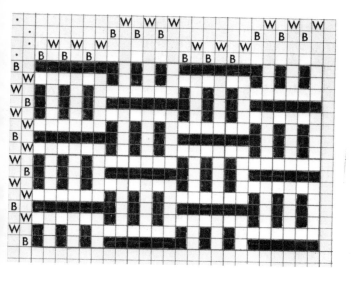

4-42. Log-cabin variation, broken herringbone threading, in fabric by Delma Kelly.
Draft for Fig. 4-42

4-43. Variation on Fig. 4-42 by Delma Kelly.

4-44. Log-cabin variation ("meander" pattern) in fabric by Takeko Nomiya.

Below:
Draft for Fig. 4-43

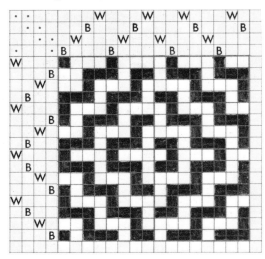

Below:
Draft for Fig. 4-44

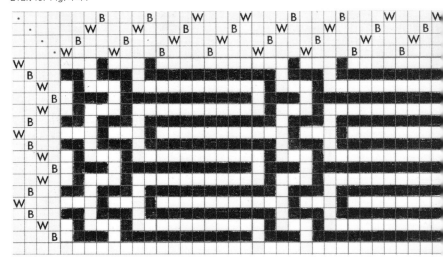

EIGHT-HARNESS TWILLS

Versatile as the four-harness loom is, eight harnesses add a wealth of possibilities to what the weaver can do. Instead of twills with only one diagonal line, several diagonals, called traces, can be woven. The eight harnesses are used as if two four-harness looms were put together.

The symbols that designate the twill traces are the same as for regular twill weaves, and the symbols are written next to each other to indicate several traces in one weave. For example, if the weave is a combination of a $2/2$ twill on the first four harnesses and a $1/3$ twill on the back four harnesses, the designation is $2/2$ $1/3$ /, meaning two warps up, two warps down; one warp up, three warps down. The tie-up for this pattern (Figure 4-45) is:

$$1\text{-}2\text{-}5$$
$$2\text{-}3\text{-}6$$
$$3\text{-}4\text{-}7$$
$$4\text{-}5\text{-}8$$
$$1\text{-}5\text{-}6$$
$$2\text{-}6\text{-}7$$
$$3\text{-}7\text{-}8$$
$$1\text{-}4\text{-}8$$

Three traces can be woven simultaneously on eight

4-45. Eight-harness twill with two traces ($2/2$ $1/3$).

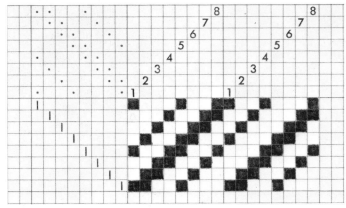

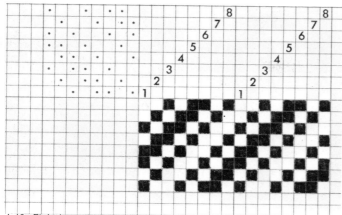

4-46. Eight-harness twill with three traces (½ ¹⁄₁ ²⁄₁).
4-47. Eight-harness point twill with three traces (½ ¹⁄₁ ²⁄₁).

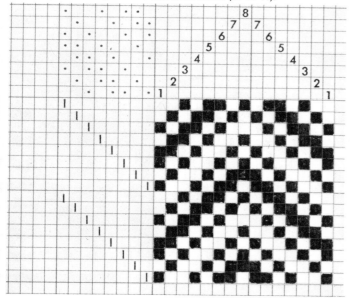

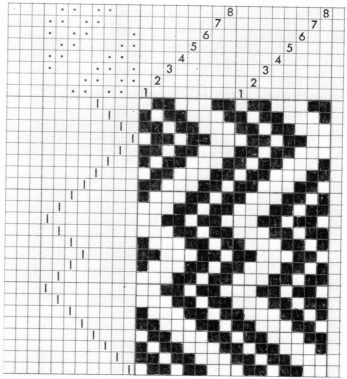

4-48. Lightning twill.

4-49. Side-by-side twills on eight harnesses.

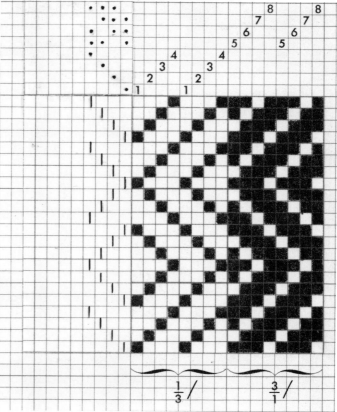

$\frac{1}{3}$ / $\frac{3}{1}$ /

harnesses also. For a ½ ¹⁄₁ ²⁄₁ twill (Figure 4-46), the tie-up is:

1-4-6-7
2-5-7-8
1-3-6-8
1-2-4-7
2-3-5-8
1-3-4-6
2-4-5-7
3-5-6-8

Balanced and unbalanced twills can be combined on an eight-harness loom; these patterns are versatile, intricate, and interesting. Two sets of twills can be threaded side by side in block patterns, using the first four harnesses for one block, the second set for another (Figure 4-49); plain and basket weaves can also be combined to form blocks (Figure 4-51). Undulating twills, broken twills, and reverse twills also give many interesting effects—Figures 4-52 and 4-53 show two of these fluid and graceful weaves.

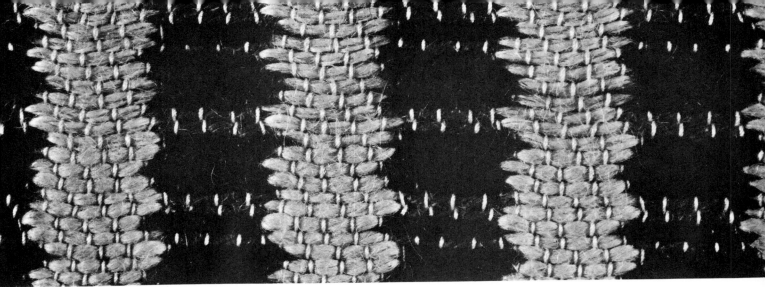

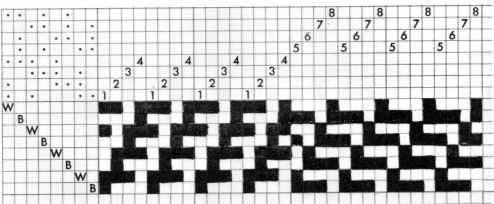

4-50. Side-by-side twills on eight harnesses in upholstery fabric by Else Regensteiner. Draft for Fig. 4-50

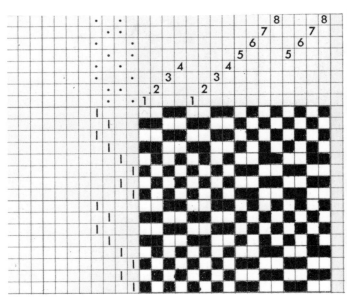

4-51. Side-by-side plain and basket weaves threaded in a block arrangement on eight harnesses.

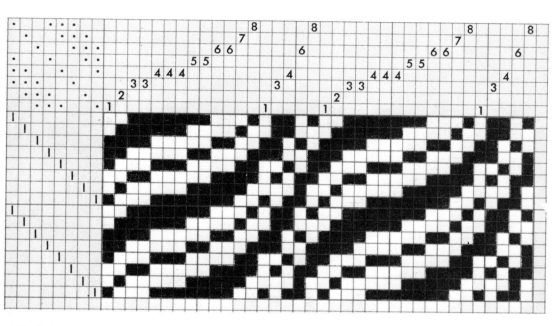

4-52. Undulating twill on eight harnesses in upholstery fabric by Else Regensteiner. Draft for Fig. 4-52

4-53. Broken twill on eight harnesses in suiting fabric by Jennifer Stewart.
Draft for Fig. 4-53

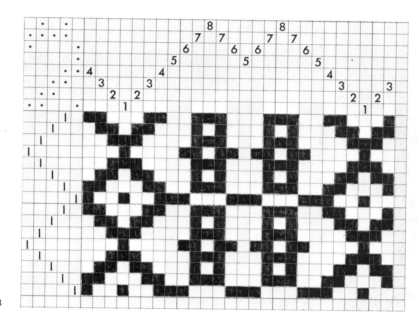

4-54. Eight-harness point twill pattern by Ruta Bremanis. Draft for Fig. 4-54

EIGHT-HARNESS COLOR PATTERNS

Eight-harness color patterns provide a wide range of design possibilities. Figures 4-55 through 4-56 show some of the variations that can be made with a setting of eight light and eight dark threads in a repeat.

A life time could be spent exploring and inventing fresh designs with the basic weaves and weaves derived from them. Design, which is a combination of mathematical precision and creative vision, is an exciting and ever new face of weaving.

4-55. Eight-harness star pattern. Draft for Fig. 4-55

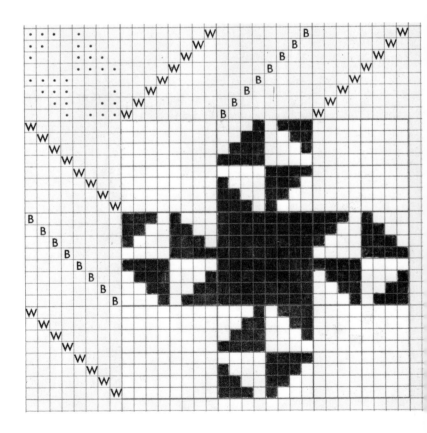

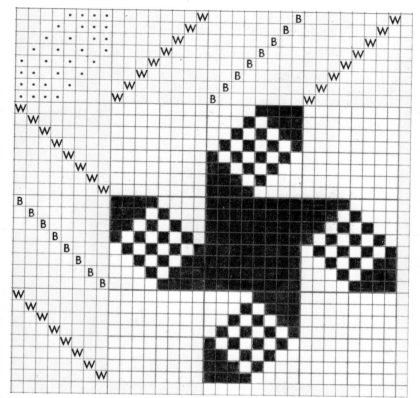

Draft for Fig. 4-56

Draft for Fig. 4-57

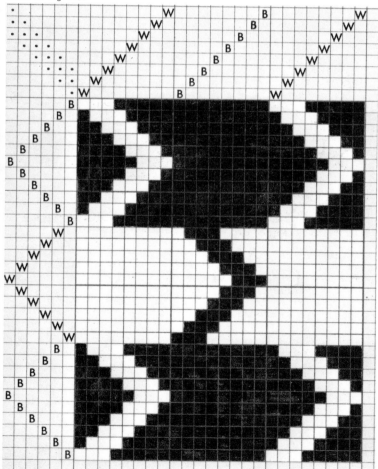

4-56. Eight-harness windmill pattern.

4-57. Eight-harness leapfrog pattern.

5

PATTERN WEAVES

Patterns are tools for designing; they widen the scope of possibilities rather than confining or limiting the weaver. A draft should never be a recipe, but serve as a basis for discovery. The following pattern weaves therefore are not meant to be mere directions to be repeated or final goals in themselves. Learning their fundamental principles should encourage the weaver to find fresh designs and applications. Once the structures of the patterns are understood, they can be adapted in new ways. Some of the weaves described are easy, some more complicated, but all have been selected because of their potential for creative adaptation.

The structure of pattern weaves is usually based on arranging the warp threads in groups, forming design units. On a four-harness loom, four threadings are standard combinations:

> harnesses 1 and 2 (threading 1,2,1,2)
> harnesses 2 and 3 (threading 2,3,2,3)
> harnesses 3 and 4 (threading 3,4,3,4)
> harnesses 1 and 4 (threading 1,4,1,4)

Each unit can be used in any sequence any number of times—the arrangement of the units is the basis of the pattern. In the weaver's language, patterns produced by this system are called "overshot," because when the harnesses are raised, the weft threads skip or "float" over the groups of warp threads.

In order to bind the floats and provide a background for them, a tabby (plain weave) must be woven between them. When a tabby is used in this way, as a binder, it is indicated on the draft by Xs to distinguish it from the pattern. The weft for the tabby is placed on a separate shuttle and should be finer in texture than the pattern threads and of a different color to enhance the effect of the pattern.

A tabby is inserted after each pattern shot and makes repetition of the same shot possible. This is very important in enlarging a pattern and in emphasizing the blocks. The first tabby, given the letter A, uses shed 1 and 3; the second tabby, given the letter B, uses shed 2 and 4. It is a great help to start tabby A always from the same side and tabby B always from the opposite side of the loom. (Attaching a small piece of masking tape to the breast beam on each side with the letters A and B written on the respective side will prevent mistakes.)

The tabby is usually taken for granted in the draft and is not mentioned or indicated every time. It is enough to give the notation "use tabby" with the draft to signify that a tabby follows each pattern pick automatically.

The tie-up for the overshot pattern commonly is the standard twill combination:

> 1-2
> 2-3
> 3-4
> 4-1

Traditionally, the treadling sequence is the same as the threading sequence and is repeated just as often. If, for example, the first threading unit is 1,2 six times, tie-up 1-2 is also used six times. If the second unit is 2,3 twice, then the treadling is 2-3 for the same number of times, and so on. This principle is called "weaving as drawn in." It results in a perfectly squared pattern. However, the modern handweaver is not compelled to adhere to strict rules and can try out treadling combinations as he pleases. An overshot pattern with a very attractive geometric design is illustrated in Figure 5-3. The pattern, composed of blocks of many different sizes in imaginative colors, transforms a traditional pattern into an excellent contemporary design. The draft shows only one repeat.

Sometimes the pattern unit does not raise and lower

5-1. Star pattern. Traditional overshot weave adapted for contemporary fabric by Benjamin Gladfelter.

5-2. Overshot pattern in upholstery fabric by Terry Albright.

the warp threads at the selvages. Therefore, a straight twill threading is commonly used for the first four threads at both sides of the warp. (This is not shown in the drafts here.)

SUMMER AND WINTER PATTERN (FOUR HARNESSES)

In contemporary weaving an especially satisfying and versatile pattern is one called Summer and Winter. The intriguing name comes from the time when coverlets were an important item in the household, and they were woven with a light-colored side used in summertime and a dark side used during the winter months. The weave produces a reversible design with the warp predominating on one side, the weft on the other. It can be woven in a multitude of variations. Because of its threading, the largest float is only over three threads at a time; for this reason it is strong enough for upholstery, drapery, and even clothing fabric.

Summer and Winter produces warp and weft blocks that are interchangeable. The threading consists of two blocks, A and B. These are threaded differently than most overshot patterns. Block A is threaded 1,3,2,3; block B is threaded 1,4,2,4. This makes it necessary to weave the tabby with tie-ups 1-2 and 3-4.

In planning the different sizes of blocks, a short, or profile, draft can be used (see Figure 5-10). A profile draft gives only the proportions of the blocks, for design purposes. When the threading has been decided, each square on the graph paper shows how many times this part of the threading will be repeated. The first line indicates block A, the second line block B, etc. (In profile drafts for large pieces, one square may represent one inch, rather than a threading group.)

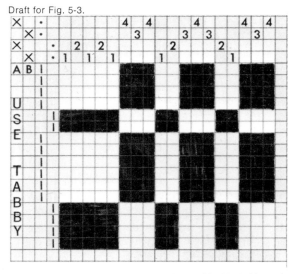

Draft for Fig. 5-3.

5-3. Overshot pattern in fabric for a bedspread by Linda Howard. The warp consists of five different shades of rose, the pattern weft of vibrant purple. The tabby is shocking pink.

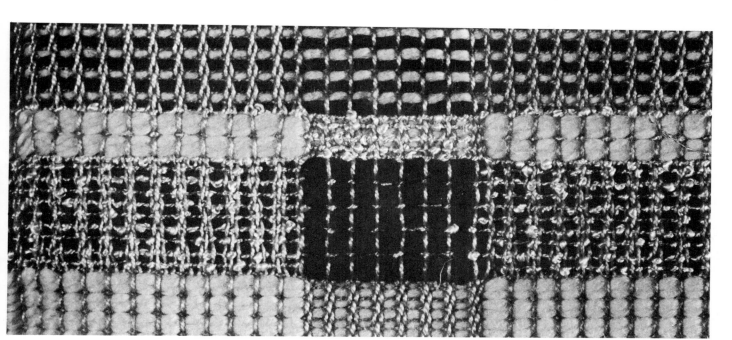

5-4. Four-harness Summer and Winter pattern showing warp and weft blocks.

5-5. Four-harness Summer and Winter pattern in upholstery fabric by Else Regensteiner. The blocks are split into different colors.

Many variations are possible with Summer and Winter. The blocks in the warp may be the same size or different sizes; the warp threads may be all the same color and texture or different colors and textures, and so on. Blocks can be split into different colors, with half a block in one color, the other half in another color. Three colors rotating in the two blocks will "throw over" each color and make it appear different in each block. For example, if the warp is threaded with block A white, block B black, block A gray, block B white, block A black, and block B gray, the resulting design will appear far more intricate than it really is.

Even more variations are possible in the weft. The tabby tie-ups for Summer and Winter are:

Tabby A—1-2
Tabby B—3-4

The pattern tie-ups are:

Block A—1-3
2-3
Block B—1-4
2-4

There are many variations in weaving, depending on the treadling. If the same pick is repeated continuously, with tabbies woven between each pattern shot, a verti-

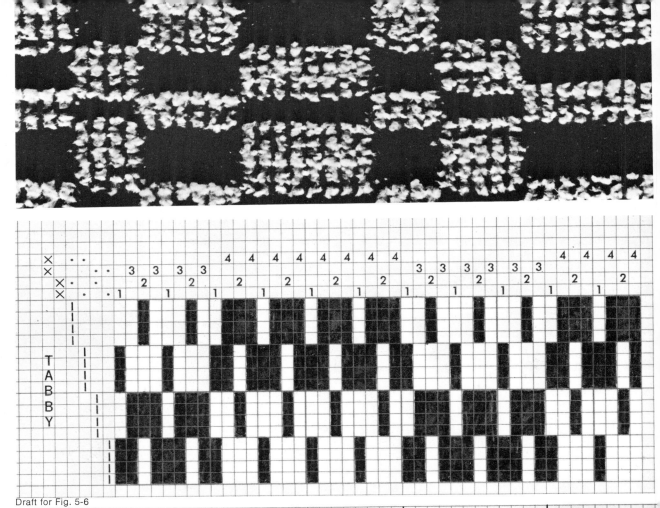

Draft for Fig. 5-6

USE TABBY

Draft for Fig. 5-7

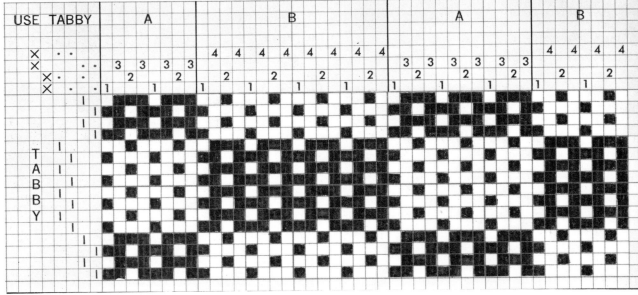

Left:
5-6. Four-harness Summer and Winter pattern by
Takeko Nomiya. The blocks are woven
in vertical lines.

cal design (Figure 5-6) is formed. If both tie-ups in the same block, with tabbies between them, are repeated continuously, a brick design (Figure 5-7) results.

Still other variations can be produced by alternating tie-ups 1-3 and 2-3 with tie-ups 1-4 and 2-4, by treadling in pairs (using a tabby only after two pattern picks), by changes in weft colors and textures, by changes in the sizes of the blocks, and so on.

If a twill treadling is used without a tabby, an allover pattern will appear instead of the blocks.

Polychrome effects can be achieved by the following treadling:

          1-3—use color A
          1-4—use color B
          2-3—use color A (or C)
          2-4—use color B (or D)

The colors in this pattern may be changed at will, but the treadling sequence must remain the same. Because the treadling uses all the threading combinations in rotation, this method can be used without a tabby after every shot. It will produce all weft blocks, as illustrated in Figure 5-8.

SUMMER AND WINTER PATTERN (EIGHT HARNESSES)

The Summer and Winter pattern on eight harnesses is a continuation of the method described for four harnesses. There is much greater scope for design, however, because the blocks do not need to be used alternately but can be combined in the weaving. In addition, six blocks are possible.

The threading for eight harnesses is:
          Block A—1,3,2,3
          Block B—1,4,2,4
          Block C—1,5,2,5
          Block D—1,6,2,6
          Block E—1,7,2,7
          Block F—1,8,2,8

These blocks may be arranged in many ways, following each other in any sequence designed beforehand by profile drafting. An example is given in Figure 5-9.

Left:
5-7. Four-harness Summer and Winter pattern by
Takeko Nomiya. The blocks here are woven
in a brick design.

5-8. Polychrome four-harness Summer and Winter pattern by Else Regensteiner.

5-9. Eight-harness Summer and Winter pattern in upholstery fabric by Else Regensteiner.

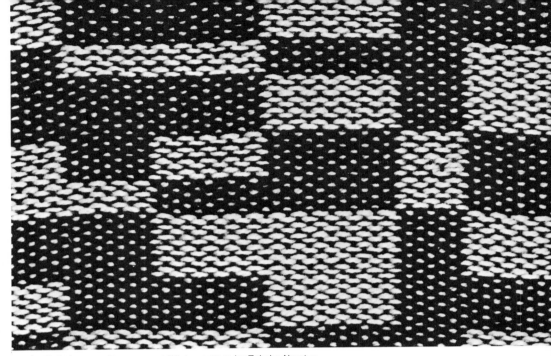

5-10. Eight-harness Summer and Winter pattern by Takeko Nomiya.

The tabby tie-ups are:
Tabby A—1-2
Tabby B—3-4-5-6-7-8

Any block harness can be used for the pattern, but it must always be raised together with either harness 1 or harness 2. The block harnesses can be used one at a time or in combination.

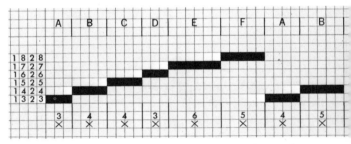

Profile draft showing size of warp blocks for Fig. 5-10 (reduced).

Profile draft for complete sample shown in Fig. 5-10 (reduced)

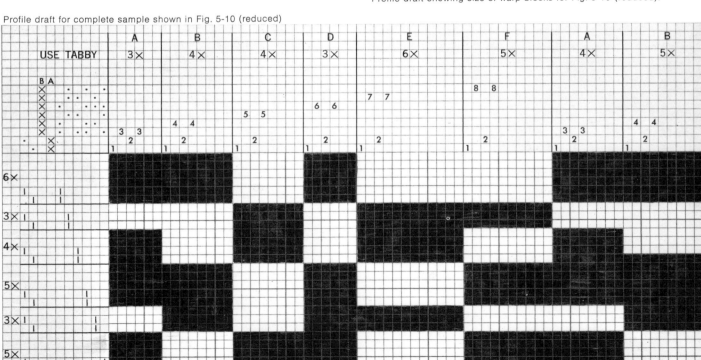

5-11. Four-harness honeycomb weave from the front (above) and back (below).

HONEYCOMB PATTERN (FOUR HARNESSES)

The honeycomb pattern is one of the rare patterns in which warp and weft need not stay perpendicular to each other. The weft may be woven in wavy lines to build circles or ovals. It has a character all its own, not being related to the diagonal of the twill or the rectangular shape of the block. Nevertheless, it is a block pattern in its threading. The honeycomb pattern is most successful when the proportions of the design are kept small, mainly because it produces a skip of weft on the reverse. Adding to its attraction is a three-dimensional effect that gives it depth and shading. Changes in the texture of the tabby, which makes the outline, can make the pattern look soft and fluffy or severe and sturdy.

The threading is:

    Block A—1,2,1,2
    Block B—3,4,3,4

The tabby tie-ups are:

    Tabby A—1-3
    Tabby B—2-4

The pattern tie-ups are:

    Block A—1-2-3
             1-2-4
    Block B—1-3-4
             2-3-4

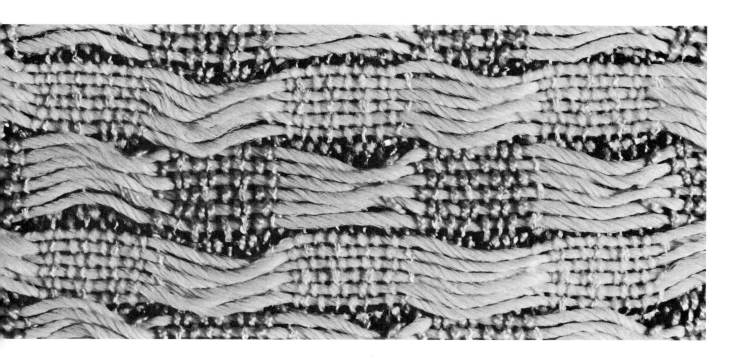

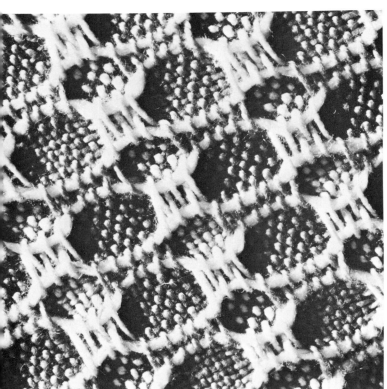

A good first sample of this weave is illustrated in Figure 5-12. It is treadled by repeating block A several times (the number of times depends on the desired size of the block), then weaving tabby A in heavy yarn, then repeating block B several times, and weaving tabby B in heavy yarn. The starting and ending of tabby and pattern picks should be arranged in the best way to

5-12. Four-harness honeycomb weave.

Draft for Fig. 5-12

5-13. Two variations of four-harness honeycomb weave by Takeko Nomiya.

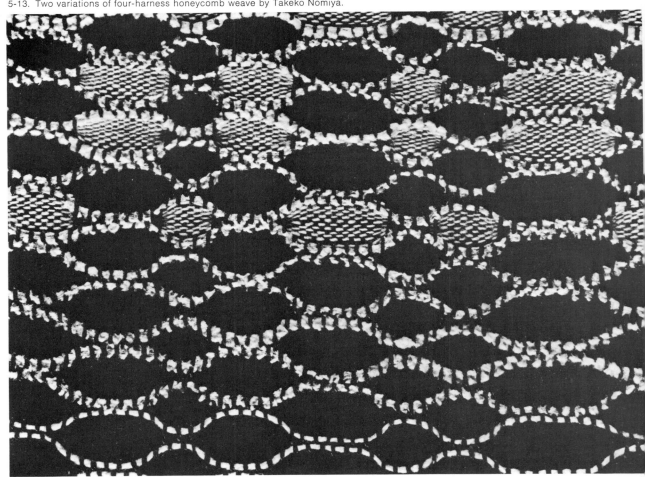

bind adjacent areas. As the tabby pulls the ovals together, the tension in warp and weft should be kept very loose.

To vary the honeycomb pattern, the size, color, and texture of the blocks can be changed. If colors are repeated in an uneven sequence, a jewel-like effect will be produced, even if only three colors are used. The tabbies can be used one at a time between blocks, or both tabbies can be used between each block, bringing four tabby yarns together at the joining point. For excellent upholstery fabric, use the tabby several times so it serves as a background thread for the ovals. This avoids long, loose warp threads and produces a smooth allover surface.

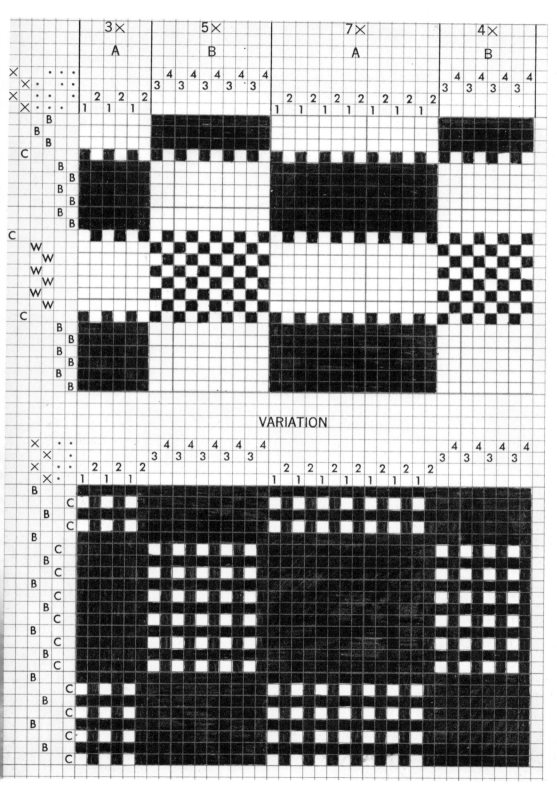

Drafts for Fig. 5-13

(B = black wool,
W = white wool,
C = heavy white chenille)

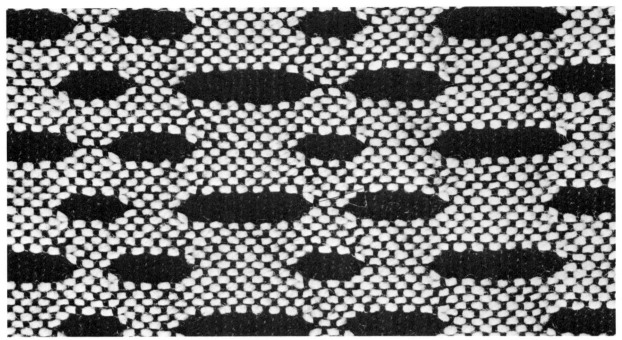

5-14. Front (above) and reverse of four-harness honeycomb pattern by Takeko Nomiya.
In the ovals the warp and weft are both black; the remaining weft is white.

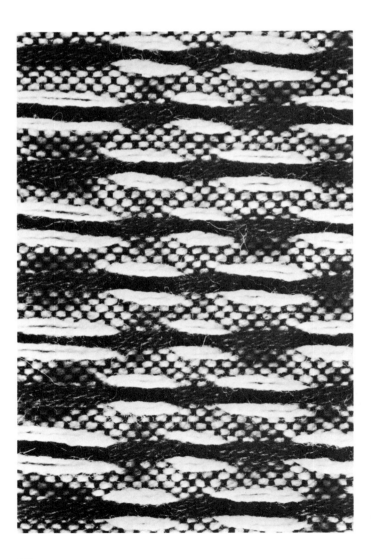

HONEYCOMB PATTERN (EIGHT HARNESSES)

When eight harnesses are used for the honeycomb pattern, the two blocks of the pattern are extended, and the result is four different blocks.

The threading is:

Block A—1,2,1,2
Block B—3,4,3,4
Block C—5,6,5,6
Block D—7,8,7,8

Each block can be repeated as often as desired.

The tabby tie-ups are:

Tabby A—1-3-5-7
Tabby B—2-4-6-8

The pattern tie-ups are:

Block A—2-3-4-5-6-7-8
1-3-4-5-6-7-8
Block B—1-2-4-5-6-7-8
1-2-3-5-6-7-8
Block C—1-2-3-4-6-7-8
1-2-3-4-5-7-8
Block D—1-2-3-4-5-6-8
1-2-3-4-5-6-7

These blocks can be repeated in any treadling sequence desired.

A number of tabbies must be woven between each block to make the design effective and practical. The sample in Figure 5-15 was made by weaving blocks A, C, B, and D with six picks of tabby between each block. Three colors were used in rotation for the four blocks so the same color was not used on the same block consecutively.

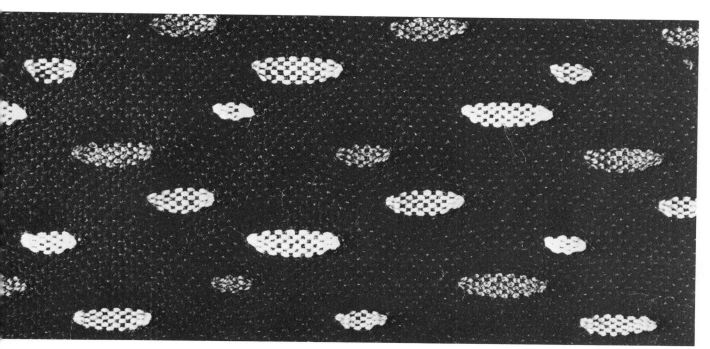

-15. Eight-harness honeycomb pattern by Takeko Nomiya. The warp is black; the weft is white, green, and turquoise for the blocks and black for the tabby.

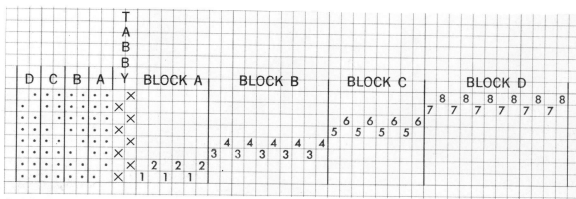

Draft for Fig. 5-15 by Eunice Anders

M AND O PATTERN

Related to the honeycomb but adding two different blocks with only four harnesses is a pattern traditionally called M and O. Its characteristic floats can be placed opposite each other or can be arranged in twill or even herringbone fashion. The tabby can contrast or blend with the pattern. If woven tightly, the floats may even be cut in the center to make tassels for decoration.

16. "Handspun," drapery fabric in M and O pattern designed for the power loom by Julia McVicker and Else Regensteiner.

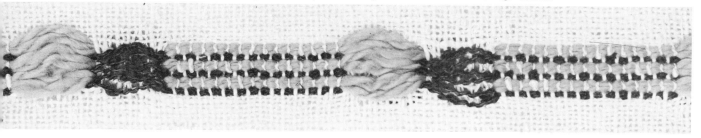

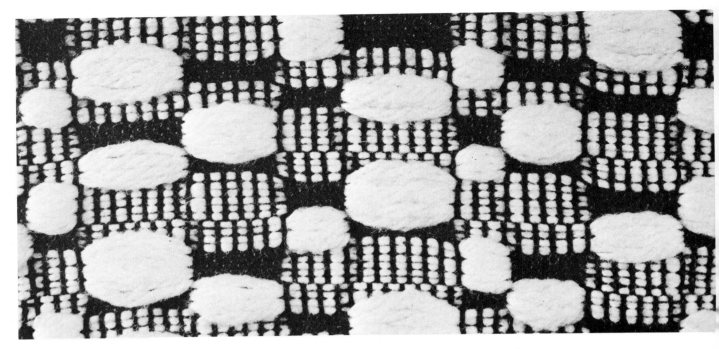

5-17. M and O pattern
by Takeko Nomiya.
Draft for Fig. 5-17

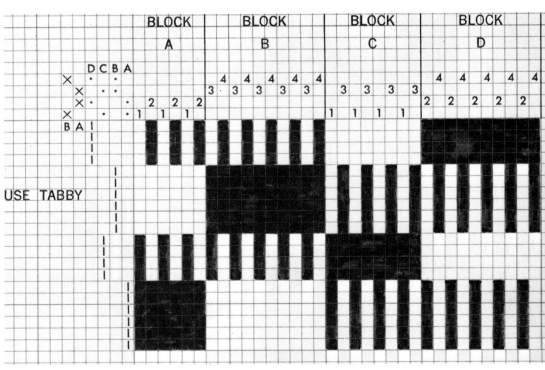

The threading for M and O is:

    Block A—1,2,1,2
    Block B—3,4,3,4
    Block C—1,3,1,3
    Block D—2,4,2,4

The tabby tie-ups are:

    Tabby A—2-3
    Tabby B—1-4

(Note that the tabby will not be "pure" because two threads will rise together where the blocks join.)

The tie-ups for the pattern are:

    Block A—1-2
    Block B—3-4
    Block C—1-3
    Block D—2-4

Each block can be built up and treadled as often as desired, with a tabby after each pattern shot.

LACE WEAVES

Woven laces fall into two categories—loom-controlled and finger-controlled weaves. Both of these are only faintly related to the original needle-and-bobbin lace techniques.

Loom-Controlled Lace Weaves

Loom-controlled lace weaves are necessarily coarser and less intricate than the twisted and knotted products of finger weaving. At the loom, lace effects can be achieved by leaving open spaces in warp and weft and by grouping threads in heddles and reed. Yarns for lace may be fine or coarse, textured or smooth. The lace may be an allover open weave, or it may be made in sections set off in blocks against plain weave, as in Figure 5-18.

5-18. Wall hanging with squares of Swedish lace by Darlyne Kasper.

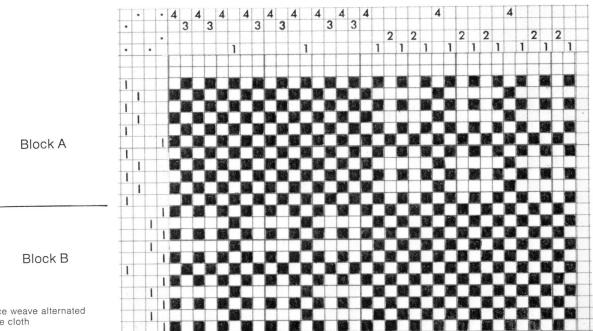

Block A

Block B

5-19. Loom-controlled lace weave alternated
with plain weave in a table cloth
by Else Regensteiner.
Draft for Fig. 5-19.

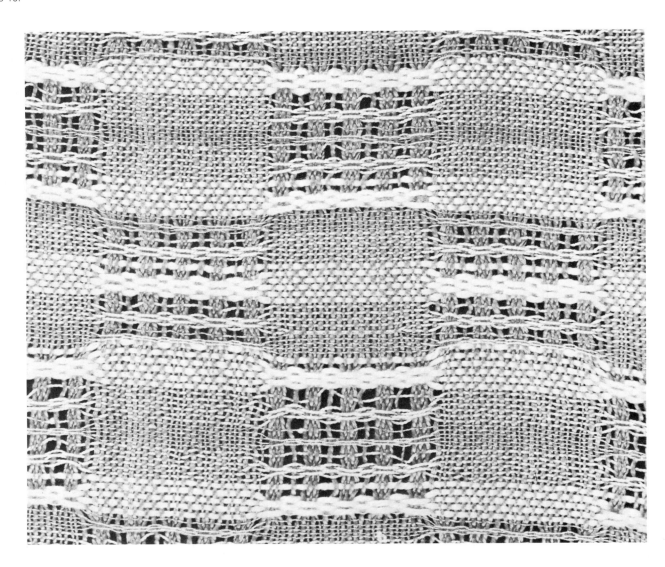

The lace shown in Figure 5-19 is woven in the typical block pattern of Swedish lace. The threading is (from right to left):

Block A—1,2,1,2,1
4
1,2,1,2,1
4
1,2,1,2,1
Block B—4,3,4,3,4
1
4,3,4,3,4
1
4,3,4,3,4

In this weave the tabby is part of the pattern. The separate threading of 4 and 1 serves as a binding; these are called the tie-down threads.

The tie-up is:

Block A— 1-3
4
1-3
4
1-3
2-4
Block B— 1-3
2-4
1
2-4
1
2-4

The blocks may be treadled as often as desired. If instead of alternating the blocks in the treadling, one block is repeated continuously, the lace units will form vertical stripes.

The pattern can be made more open by threading groups of threads through a single dent and leaving a dent free on each side of the tie-down threads. This kind of sleying can produce allover lace such as that shown in Figure 5-20. This pattern is threaded:

4,3,4
2,4
2,1,2
4,2
4,3,4 (sleyed through the same dent)
0,2,0 (open dent on each side)
0,4,0 (open dent on each side)
2,1,2 (sleyed through the same dent)
0,4,0 (open dent on each side)
0,2,0 (open dent on each side)

The tie-ups and treadling are:

2-3
3-4 } beat together
2-3

1-4
2-3

1-2
1-4 } beat together
1-2

2-3
1-4

A great deal depends on the adjustment of the beat to achieve an open structure.

An enlarged version of lace weave can be worked out for eight harnesses. An example is given in Figure 5-21.

5-20. Allover lace weave with threads of various textures.

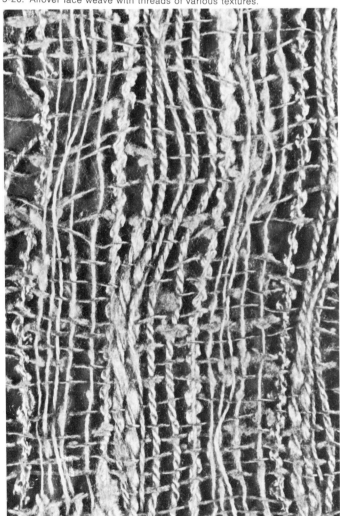

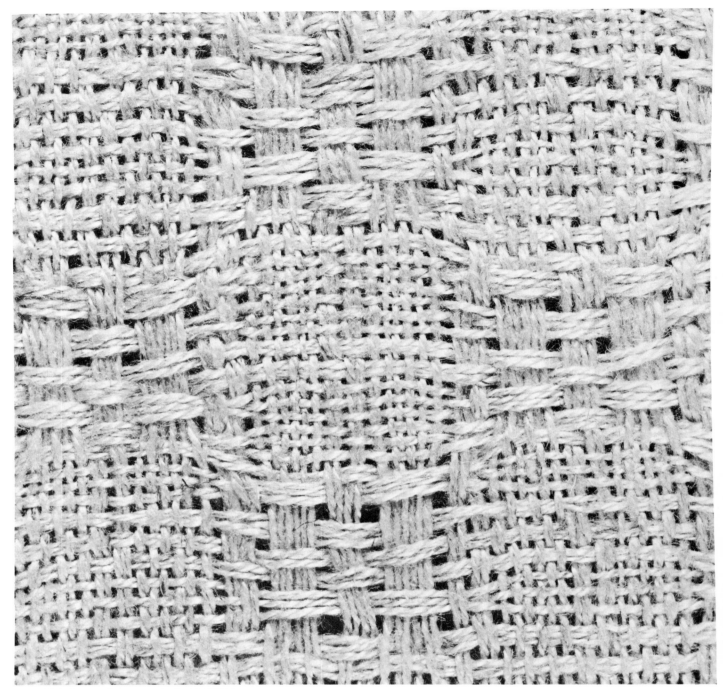

5-21. Eight-harness lace weave by Lurene Stone.

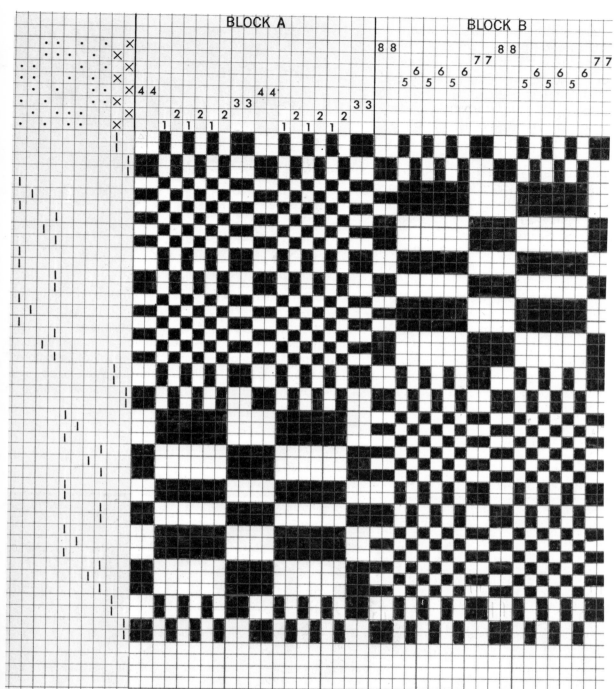

Draft for Fig. 5-21

Finger-Controlled Lace Weaves

Greek mythology tells of Arachne, a weaver who wove such beautiful cloth that the goddess Athena became jealous and challenged her to a contest. Arachne's weaving so far surpassed that of Athena that the goddess became furious and destroyed Arachne's work. In despair, Arachne tried to hang herself, but the remorseful goddess changed the rope into a cobweb and Arachne into a spider, so that she could weave perfect webs forever.

Perhaps no other weave comes closer to Arachne's delicate webs than fine finger-controlled lace. Among the most exquisite examples are those produced by the weavers of ancient Peru; an example of a Peruvian gauze weave is shown in Figure 5-22.

Finger-controlled lace weaves are especially personal creations. The sensitivity of the hand, not the mechanics of the loom, produces an intimate relationship between material and conception, technique and response. Any loom that makes a plain weave can be used, and the technique is therefore excellent for the two-harness loom.

Threads stretched on the loom may be twisted and braided, tied and wrapped, interlocked and opened up with spaces and intervals, and woven in a multitude of intricate-seeming designs.

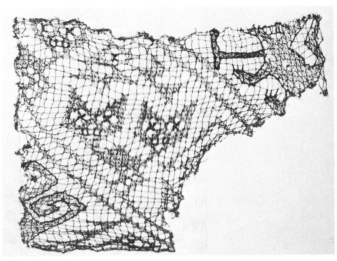

5-22. Peruvian gauze from Chancay, made about 900 A.D. (Photo courtesy of the Art Institute of Chicago)

Open spacing in the reed can produce a simple airy weave. Threads may be doubled or tripled in some dents and skipped entirely in others, while the gentle adjustment of the beat and manipulation of the yarns with the fingers or a comb bring about quite different effects. Additions of various materials, such as pebbles, seashells, or other objects, show to best advantage in these fine transparent webs.

5-23. "Wall Hanging with Sea-Stars," lace weave of unspun wool, linen, and rayon by Else Regensteiner.

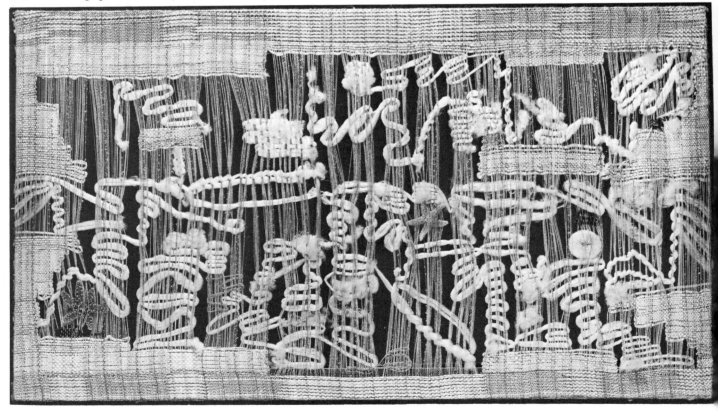

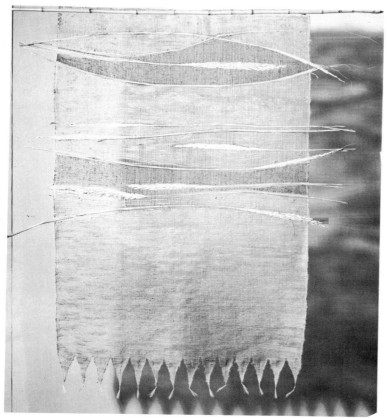

5-24. "Florida I," transparent weave of silk, linen, and sea oats by Diane Wiersba. (Photo courtesy of the artist)

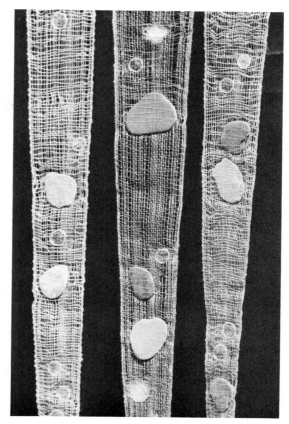

5-25. "Pebbles," detail of transparent wall hanging with slate pebbles inserted in woven pockets of natural linen warp by Theo Moorman. (Photo courtesy of the artist)

Gauze Weaves

Gauze, or leno, weave can produce extremely delicate lace. In this weave the warp threads are twisted around each other and secured by the weft thread. A small, smooth pick-up stick (Figure 5-26) and a flat shuttle must be used.

5-26. Pick-up stick.

5-27. Gauze or leno weave.

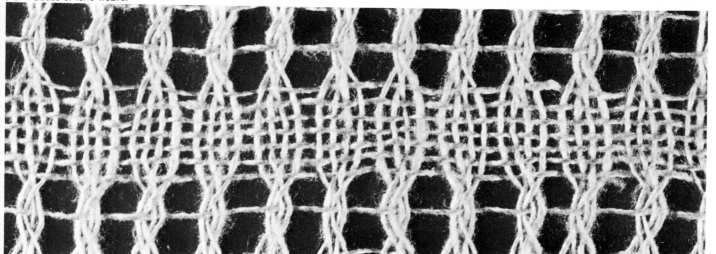

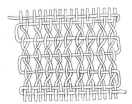

5-28. Leno technique.

The procedure, illustrated in Figure 5-28, is as follows:

(1) Weave several rows of plain weave.

(2) Starting on the right side of the loom, open the plain-weave shed so that the first thread is on the bottom. With the pick-up stick, push aside the first thread on the top and pick up the first thread below. Keep this on the stick while going over the next thread on top to pick up the next thread below. This makes the twist. Continue this twisting process to the other side of the warp.

(3) Turn the pick-up stick on its edge so that it makes an opening between the twisted threads. Guide the shuttle through this opening, securing the weft at the beginning so it will not pull out.

(4) Remove the pick-up stick and beat the weft lightly and carefully.

(5) Change to the other plain-weave shed. Weave with the same shuttle and weft through this shed, with-out twists, returning to the right side of the warp. Beat lightly.

(6) Change shed again and repeat the pick-up from the start.

This technique can be varied in many ways. Instead of one thread, a group of threads can be twisted. In the second pick-up row, the warp threads may be divided and other groups may be picked up. Solid plain weave may be woven between the rows of leno. The weave may also be made with the shed closed and the groups of warp threads twisted around each other.

Spanish Lace

For Spanish lace weave, illustrated in Figure 5-30, the procedure is this:

(1) Start on the left side of the warp. With a small shuttle, weave a small group of warp threads in plain weave, going back and forth as often as desired.

(2) Carry the weft to the next group of warp threads and weave this group as many times as the first in plain weave. Continue until all groups are woven across the loom.

(3) When the shuttle reaches the right side, the same groups can be woven the same way in the opposite direction. The thread that connects them will then form an additional design.

Many interesting variations on this pattern can be made by changing the groups of warp threads, varying the number of threads in the groups, or alternating and splitting the groups.

5-29. Gauze weave in a wall hanging by Jane Redman.

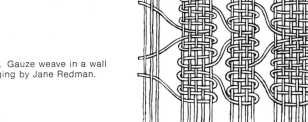

5-30. Spanish lace technique.

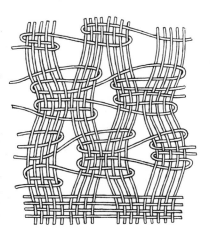

5-31. Spanish lace in vertical and split arrangement.

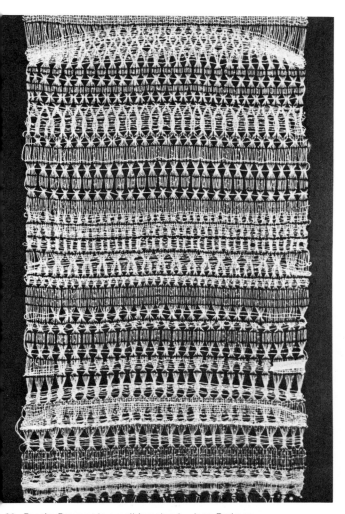

5-32. Brooks Bouquet in a wall hanging by Jane Redman.

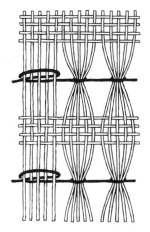

5-33. Brooks Bouquet technique.

Detail of Fig. 5-32

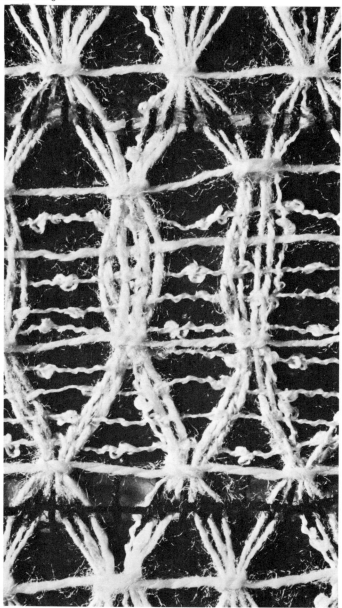

Brooks Bouquet

Grouping and tying warp threads is another ancient lace technique. The so-called Brooks Bouquet is an easy and handsome example of this technique. Illustrated in Figure 5-33, it is woven as follows:

(1) Weave several picks of plain weave.

(2) Open a plain-weave shed and bring the shuttle out at the spot where the first bouquet is planned (after five threads in the example shown).

(3) Take the shuttle over the top back to where it started. Bring it around behind the five threads and out through the loop made by the weft. Pull tightly to make a knot.

(4) Insert shuttle in the shed again and repeat the process with the next group of threads. Repeat until all desired bouquets are woven; keep the shed open all the time.

(5) Change to the other shed and weave an odd number of threads in plain weave. This will bring the shuttle to the right side again, and a new row of bouquets can be started, completing the design unit.

Danish Medallion

The Danish Medallion pattern is a very flexible design that can be produced in many different ways. One method, which requires two shuttles, one with heavy yarn and one with fine yarn (Figure 5-34), is this:

(1) Weave a few rows in plain weave.

(2) Open the next shed. Lay in a heavy weft thread from left to right.

(3) Weave several picks of plain weave in the fine yarn.

(4) Open the next shed and bring the heavy weft from the right to where the first medallion is desired. Bring the shuttle up out of the shed.

(5) With a finger or crochet hook, bring a loop of the heavy yarn over the plain weave and under the first heavy weft. Pass the shuttle through this loop and draw tightly the knot that has been formed.

(6) Pass the shuttle through the shed to the next medallion and repeat the procedure. Continue until the heavy weft thread reaches the other side of the wrap.

(7) Change the shed and bring the heavy weft to the

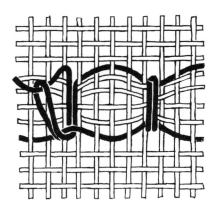

5-34. Danish Medallion technique.

right, where it will be picked up after the next set of fine plain-weave threads have been woven.

The finger-controlled lace weaves do not strictly belong to the category of pattern weaves, but they are indispensable additions to the weaver's store of techniques. Figures 5-35 through 5-37 are only a sampling of the design possibilities offered by imaginative combination of the lace techniques described here.

5-35. Sample showing (from top to bottom): Danish Medallion, Spanish lace, Brooks Bouquet, by Carolyn Saberniak.

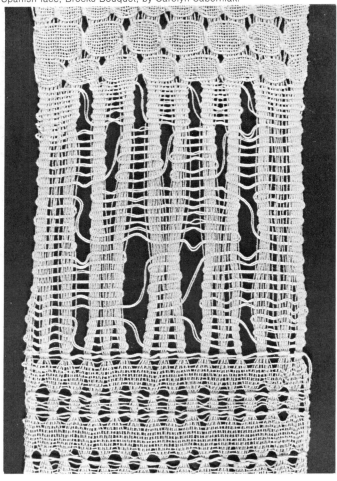

5-36. Wall hanging of jute yarns in Danish Medallion, leno, loops, and plain weave by Shelley Christensen.

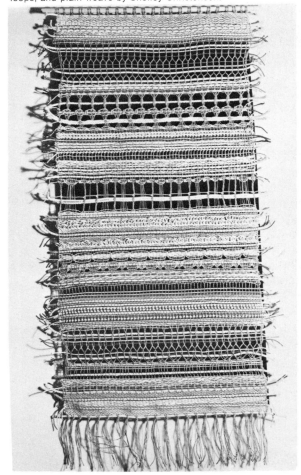

5-37. "Golden Lace," wall hanging of linen,
mohair, and silk ribbon woven in Brooks Bouquet
and Danish Medallion by Else Regensteiner.

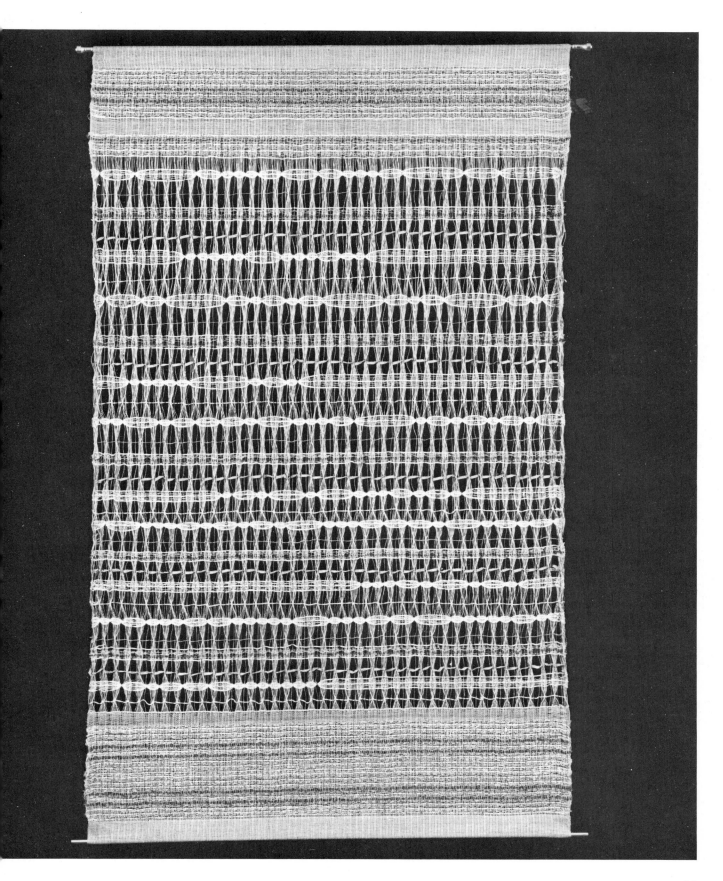

6

DOUBLE WEAVES

Double-weave cloth consists of two layers of fabric woven simultaneously, one on top of the other. The layers may be joined or separate, and designs are made by interchanging threads from the layers. The system of double weave is intriguing, and its uses are manifold. By the same system, three- and even four-layered fabric can be made.

TWO-LAYERED FABRIC (FOUR HARNESSES)

The two layers of double weave are threaded and woven on the same loom, but they are treated as two entities: half of the warp threads are threaded on two harnesses, the other half on the other two harnesses. (Since two harnesses are used to weave each layer, the only structure that can be woven double on a four-harness loom is plain weave.)

The warp is set up in the usual manner, but the colors for each layer are generally different (in order to bring out the design). In addition, the number of warp threads per inch must be doubled. Thus, if fifteen threads per inch are needed for one layer, thirty threads to the inch are required for both layers. The warp should, however, consist of an odd number of threads to prevent two adjacent threads at the edges from being woven alike.

The warp threads may be arranged with either two light and two dark threads alternating or with one light and one dark thread alternating (Figure 6-1). The threading is straight twill threading in both cases. For the sake of clarity, only single alternating white and black threads are used in the instructions given here.

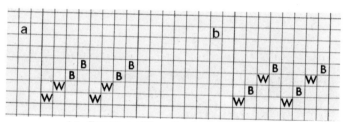

6-1. Two ways of threading for double weave.

The threading of the heddles is:

 harnesses 1 and 3—white
 harnesses 2 and 4—black

The tie-up of the treadles is:

 treadle 1 tied to harness 1
 treadle 2 tied to harness 2
 treadle 3 tied to harness 3
 treadle 4 tied to harness 4

Thus, treadles 1 and 3 raise the white threads; treadles 2 and 4 raise the black threads.

The threads are single in each heddle. The reed is sleyed with two threads (one white, one black) in each dent, except at the sides: here the sleying varies depending on the kind of double weave desired.

The method of weaving depends on the purpose for which the fabric is planned. By changing the action of the shuttle (or shuttles), fabric may be woven in tubular form (the two layers connected on both sides), in layers connected on one side only, in two separate layers, in layers connected by a "pick-up" design, or in an open top layer with a "free" design connected at intervals to the bottom layer, which serves as a background.

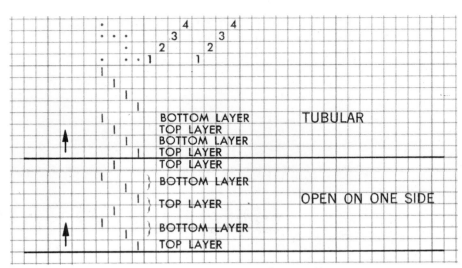

6-3. Draft for tubular weave and double weave connected on one side

The draft shows a grid with numbers 1, 2, 3, 4 and labels:

TUBULAR
BOTTOM LAYER
TOP LAYER
BOTTOM LAYER
TOP LAYER

TOP LAYER
} BOTTOM LAYER
} TOP LAYER   OPEN ON ONE SIDE
} BOTTOM LAYER
TOP LAYER

6-2. Tubular double weave.

Right:
6-4. Dress made in tubular double weave by Diane White.

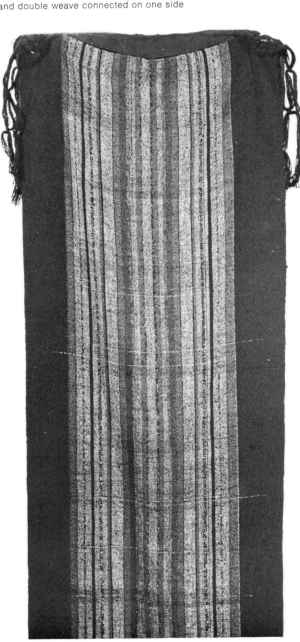

Tubular Double Weave

Tubular double weave is particularly useful for such diverse items as pillow covers, bags, ties, dresses, and wall hangings, especially three-dimensional pieces. The textures and colors to be used in the warp must be planned at the outset for both layers, but weft variations can be introduced spontaneously during the course of weaving.

In tubular double weave, the top and bottom layers are woven alternately. The threads of the top layer always stay above the threads for the bottom layer. Actually, only half of each layer is woven at a time: in order to weave the bottom layer, the whole top layer plus half of the bottom layer is raised. The weft yarn, on one shuttle, goes round and round from the top to the bottom layer in rotation.

To keep the joined edges from becoming too tight, the first and last three dents in the reed are sleyed with one thread each.

The rotation of the shuttle, or treadling sequence, is:

     1   (first pick of the top layer)
  1-2-3 (first pick of the bottom layer)
     3   (second pick of the top layer)
  1-3-4 (second pick of the bottom layer)

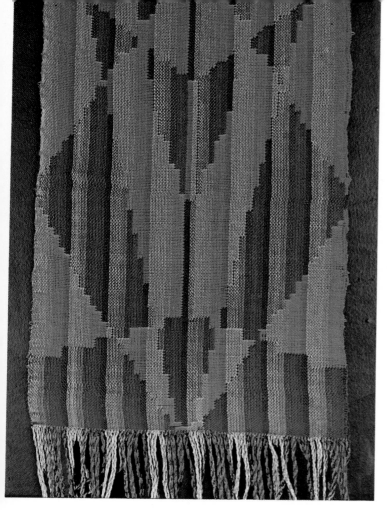

Wall hanging in double weave by Roanne Katz.

Detail showing color changes in a
double-weave fabric by Roanne Katz.

6-5. Three-dimensional hanging in tubular double weave by Lois Lebov. The tubular sections are stuffed with cotton.

6-6. Detail of a three-dimensional hanging in tubular double weave with ceramic forms by Joel W. Plum. (Photo: Don Williams)

Two-Layered Fabric Connected on One Side

When two-layered fabric that is connected on one side is taken off the loom, it unfolds to make double-width material. Thus, this method of double weave is useful for large projects such as bedspreads and tablecloths as well as for smaller projects when only a very narrow loom is available.

Since the side from which the shuttle starts is the side where the layers are *not* connected, plan which side you intend to start from in advance. The connected side should be sleyed with single threads in the last three dents, while the open side (the selvages) should be double-sleyed.

The treadling sequence is:

       1   (first pick of the top layer)
     1-2-3   (first pick of the bottom layer)
     1-3-4   (second pick of the bottom layer)
       3   (second pick of the top layer)

This rotation is then repeated from the start.

6-7. Double-weave cloth with layers connected on one side.

Two Layers Woven Separately

Weaving two unconnected layers of fabric in double weave is generally used for making two items at once —place mats, for instance—or for making three-dimensional hangings in which the layers are connected only at intervals. The two layers are woven separately by using a different shuttle for each one, but the treadling is the same as for either the tubular or edge-connected method.

Remember to sley the last three dents on each side double for selvages on both layers.

Double Weave with Pick-Up Design

For double weave with a pick-up design, the warps *must* be threaded in different colors. The design appears in the reverse color on the reverse of the fabric; that is, if the design is black on a white background on the front, it will be white on a black background on the other side.

The design should be worked out on graph paper, with filled-in squares representing the design. Each square may represent several warp threads, depending on the scale of the drawing.

Two shuttles are used: one wound with each color. In addition, a pick-up stick is needed. It should be longer than the width of the warp, and about one inch high.

The weaving procedure is as follows:

(1) Treadle 2 and 4 to raise all the black warp threads. With the beater at rest position (away from you), slide the point of the pick-up stick from the right over and under the black warp threads, picking up all design threads indicated in the first (bottom) row of the graph-paper plan. Continue until the full length of the stick is inserted in the warp. This will give you the black design on the white background. Then slide the stick with its picked up threads back against the reed, letting it ride on top of the shed. Release treadles.

(2) Treadle 1 to raise the first half of the white layer. Weave with white weft. Beat with the stick left in place; then slide the stick back against the reed again. Release treadle.

(3) Treadle 3 to raise the other half of the white warp threads. Weave white. Take out the pick-up stick and beat neatly. Use special care to get a good edge and leave a wide arc of weft in the shed so that the edges will not draw in.

(4) Treadle 1 and 3 to raise all the white warp threads. With the stick, pick up the background threads indicated in the graph (which were just woven), again working from right to left. Omit the first and last white thread in each space between the groups of black design threads. (This splitting of pairs adjoining the design is a Scandinavian technique that makes the fabric exactly reversible.) Release treadles.

(5) Treadle 2 and weave black, beating as well as possible with the pick-up stick in position. Slide stick back against the reed. Release treadle.

(6) Treadle 4 and weave black. Remove pick-up stick and beat. This completes one set of pick-up. If the woven design does not make a square with two picks in each layer for each row of the graph, use as many sets of the same picks as necessary.

(7) Continue with sets of pick-ups, changing the threads picked up according to the graph paper.

In summary, the treadling sequence of double weave with pick-up design is:

    2-4 (pick up pattern—black warp)
      1 (weave white)
      3 (weave white)
    1-3 (pick up background—white warp—splitting
         pairs on each side of design)
      2 (weave black)
      4 (weave black)

6-8, 6-9. "Machinery," hanging in double weave with pick-up design by Ulla-May Berggren. The color scheme of the design (top) is reversed on the back. (Photos courtesy of Marna Johnson)

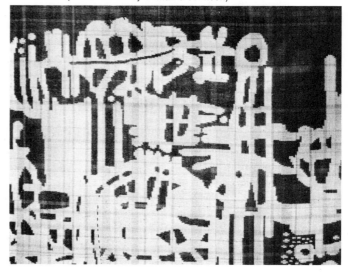

Left:
6-10, 6-11. "The Signs of the Zodiac," hanging in double weave with pick-up design by Joni Clayton. The crab is shown in detail.

6-12. "The City," hanging in double weave with pick-up design by Natalie Novotny. The design areas are stuffed with yarn. (Photo: Brand Studio)

Double Weave with Free Design

When the two layers of a double weave are threaded in different colors, and hand-controlled lace weaves are woven on the top layer, unusual and beautiful effects can be achieved. One of the advantages of this technique is its simplicity; in addition, it gives the weaver an opportunity to create complementary backgrounds for open weaves. Two examples of this technique are illustrated in color on pages 166 and 167.

The weave is made by raising the threads of the top layer, which remain unwoven, while the bottom layer is woven. When the desired background has been built up, the top layer is woven. At intervals, both layers are connected, either by weaving a plain weave with all four harnesses or by exchanging the layers, bringing the bottom warp up to act as the top warp.

6-13. "The Birds," hanging in double weave with pick-up design by Gwynne Lott.

6-14. "Squares," hanging in double weave with pick-up design by Else Regensteiner.

6-15. "Ovals," hanging in double weave with open design in top layer by Else Regensteiner.

THREE-LAYERED FABRIC (SIX HARNESSES)

Weaving three-layered fabric is an ambitious project that is particularly useful for making very wide pieces (triple the width of the warp) or three-dimensional hangings. By leaving all layers unconnected, three separate pieces may be made at once. Since each layer is woven on two harnesses, six harnesses are necessary.

For three-layered fabric, three times as many warp threads per inch are needed as for a single layer. Thus, if one layer calls for fifteen ends per inch, three layers will require forty-five threads per inch. For experimentation, you should thread each layer with a different color. A sample threading is:

harnesses 1 and 4—white (first layer)
harnesses 2 and 5—black (second layer)
harnesses 3 and 6—red (third layer)

As for two-layered fabric, only one shuttle is used if the layers are to be connected. If the layers are to be separate, a different shuttle is used for each one.

The treadling sequence is:

1	(first pick of the first layer)
1-2-4	(first pick of the second layer)
1-2-3-4-5	(first pick of the third layer)
1-2-4-5-6	(second pick of the third layer)
1-4-5	(second pick of the second layer)
4	(second pick of the first layer)

Remember that to weave the second layer you must raise all the threads of the first layer plus half those of the second layer. To weave the third layer, you must raise all the threads of the first and second layers plus half those of the third layer.

6-16. Three-layered fabric, connected and unconnected.

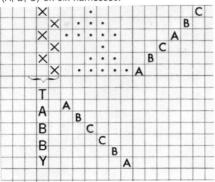

6-17. Draft for three-layered fabric. Three colors (A, B, C) on six harnesses.

FOUR-LAYERED FABRIC (EIGHT HARNESSES)

The double-weave system can also be applied to weaving four layers of fabric. Since each layer is woven on two harnesses, an eight-harness loom is needed.

This form of double weave presents a multitude of possibilities for design. The three-dimensional hanging shown in Figure 6-19 makes use of simple combinations to create an intricate-looking structure. Two warp beams were used to help control the tension of the various layers. The four layers, each a different color, were woven separately in some sections; at one point they were merged into three layers, and in other sections they were united in a single, multicolored plain weave.

6-18. Draft for four-layered fabric. Four colors (A, B, C, D) on eight harnesses.

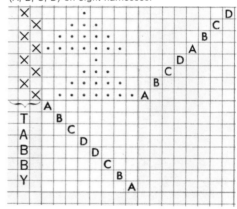

6-19. Three-dimensional hanging in four-layered weave by Joel W. Plum. (Photo courtesy of the artist)

DOUBLE-WEAVE TWILLS AND EIGHT-HARNESS PLAIN WEAVE

In the double-weave fabrics described in the first part of this chapter, only plain weave and related weave constructions are possible because only two harnesses are used for each layer. With an eight-harness loom, however, two-layered twills and pattern weaves as well as plain weaves are possible.

When twills are woven with one side connected, it is necessary to note the direction in which the twill lines will run when the fabric is unfolded and to adjust the treadling if the lines are to be continuous.

As with other double weaves, the reed should be sleyed with one thread in the last three dents on the connected sides, and selvage sides should be double-sleyed.

The threading may be arranged in one of three ways: all one color in a straight twill threading; two light and two dark colors with one color on harnesses 1,2,5, and 6 and the other color on harnesses 3,4,7,8; or alternating light and dark colors with one on harnesses 1,3,5, and 7 and the other on harnesses 2,4,6, and 8.

The following examples use the third arrangement: the top layer (harnesses 1,3,5,7) is light, the bottom layer (harnesses 2,4,6,8) is dark. The treadling is used as though there were two different warps, one for each layer. Remember that the top layer is on top of the warp; to get to the bottom layer, you must raise the whole top layer plus the part of the bottom layer that will not be woven in the pick.

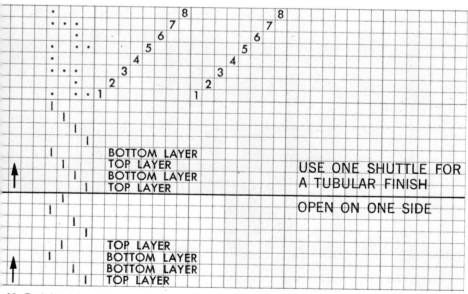

-20. Draft for eight-harness double weave in tabby.

For a tubular ²⁄₂ twill, the treadling sequence is:

1-3	(top layer)
1-2-3-4-5-7	(bottom layer)
3-5	(top layer)
1-2-3-5-7-8	(bottom layer)
5-7	(top layer)
1-3-5-6-7-8	(bottom layer)
1-7	(top layer)
1-3-4-5-6-7	(bottom layer)

For ²⁄₂ twill connected on one side with the direction of the twill lines continuous, the treadling sequence is:

1-3	(top layer)
1-2-3-4-5-7	(bottom layer)
1-2-3-5-7-8	(bottom layer)
3-5	(top layer)
5-7	(top layer)
1-3-5-6-7-8	(bottom layer)
1-3-4-5-6-7	(bottom layer)
1-7	(top layer)

For a tubular plain weave on eight harnesses, the treadling sequence is:

1-5	(top layer)
1-2-3-5-6-7	(bottom layer)
3-7	(top layer)
1-3-4-5-7-8	(bottom layer)

For a two-layered fabric connected on one side in plain weave, the treadling sequence is:

1-5	(top layer)
1-2-3-5-6-7	(bottom layer)
1-3-4-5-7-8	(bottom layer)
3-7	(top layer)

6-21. Three-panel wall hanging in eight-harness double weave with surface floats by Diane Wiersba. (Photo courtesy of the artist)

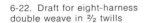

6-22. Draft for eight-harness double weave in ²⁄₂ twills

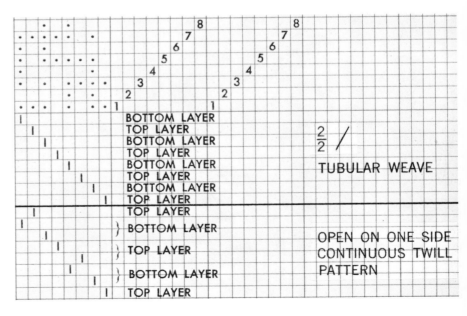

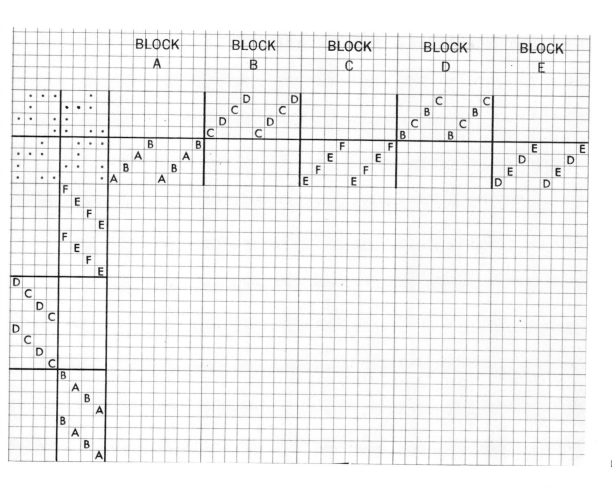

PATTERNS IN DOUBLE WEAVE

It is easy to make a checkerboard double weave by the pick up-method on a four-harness loom, but it is faster and a challenge to weave it on eight harnesses. Eight harnesses make possible double weaves in all kinds of patterns, including block and color patterns.

The checkerboard pattern, illustrated in Figure 6-23, is a side-by-side block threading with alternating colors on the harnesses. The blocks may be the same size or different sizes. The colors should alternate in light and dark and can be rearranged in the blocks. In Figure 6-23, six different colors are indicated for warp and weft.

A pattern that has only two alternating colors in either warp or weft is illustrated in Figures 6-24 and 6-25. Black and white alternate: all black threads are threaded through the first two harnesses, all white threads are on the pattern harnesses. Note that the first two harnesses serve as the binding tabbies. Each pattern combination is always used first together with harness 1, then again with harness 2, in alternating weft colors. As long as this system is followed, any harness combination can be used.

6-23. Eight-harness double weave block pattern. Six colors were used.

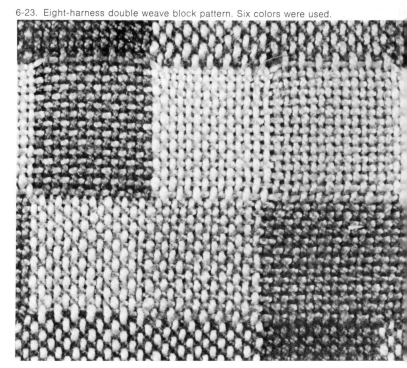

111

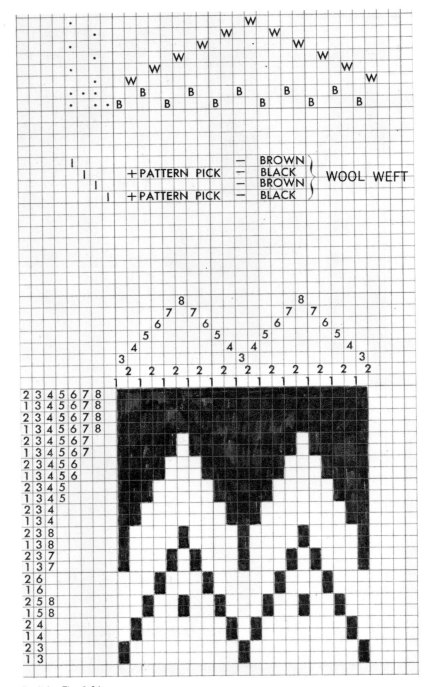

+ PATTERN PICK — BROWN
— BLACK
— BROWN } WOOL WEFT
+ PATTERN PICK — BLACK

Draft for Fig. 6-24.

6-24. Patterned eight-harness double weave.

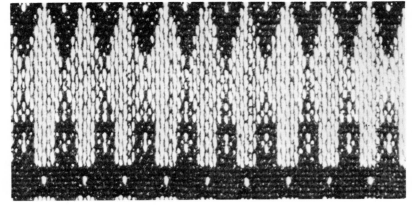

6-25. Patterned eight-harness double weave in drapery panel by Lurene Stone and Helena Jacobson.

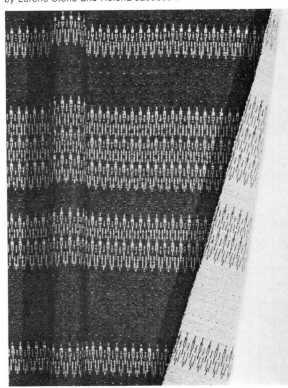

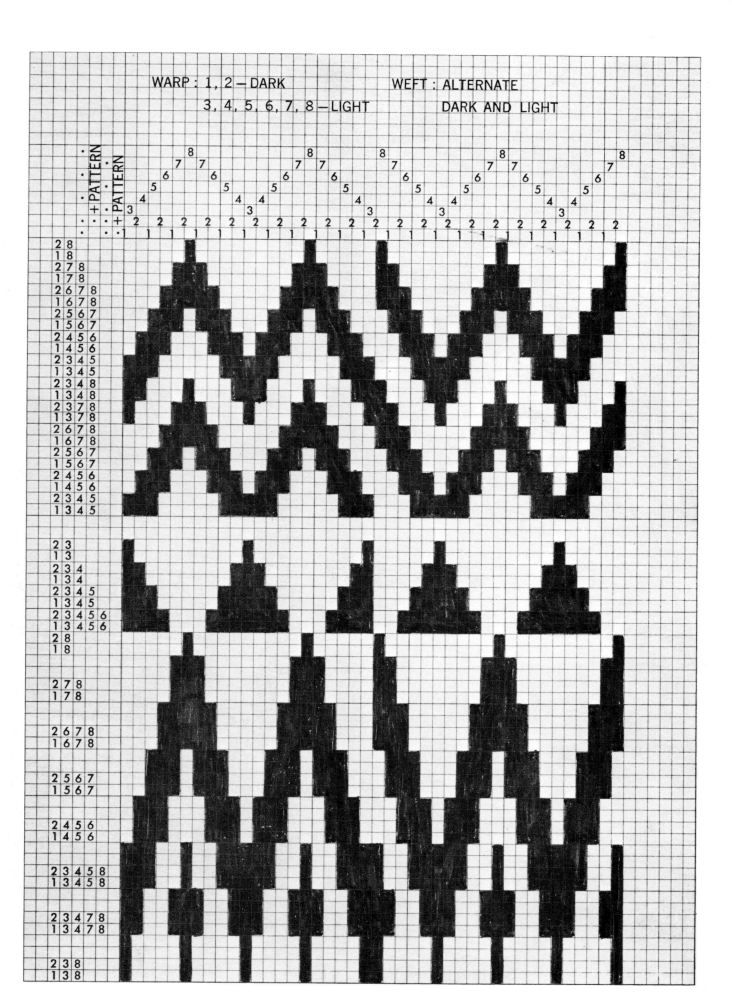

Wall hanging in double weave with
pick-up design by Darlyne Kasper.

Wall hanging in double weave by Michi Ouchi.

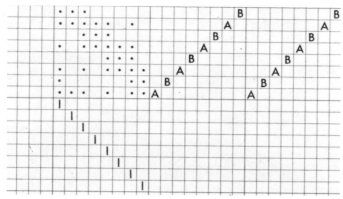

6-27. Draft for a ruana weave. For the warp, alternate A and B;
for the weft, use color A or B or alternate A and B.

STITCHED TWILL

Another double weave made on eight harnesses is warp-faced on both sides, with the two layers closely connected and interwoven. It can be seen in beautiful shawls of brushed sheep and mohair wool, called ruanas, from South America. The ruanas typically have very colorful stripes on one side and a solid color on the other.

The heavily brushed nap of the ruanas makes analysis of the weave very difficult, but the following directions from *The Handloom Weaves* are borrowed with the kind permission of the author, the late Harriet Tidball. They are illustrated in Figure 6-27.

The threading is:

      harnesses 1,3,5,7—color A

      harnesses 2,4,6,8—color B

The treadling sequence is:

    1-2-3   (top layer)

  1-2-3-4-5-7   (bottom layer)

    3-4-5   (top layer)

 1-3-4-5-6-7   (bottom layer)

    5-6-7   (top layer)

 1-3-5-6-7-8   (bottom layer)

    1-7-8   (top layer)

 1-2-3-5-7-8   (bottom layer)

If, instead of weaving warp stripes, plaid or weft stripes are desired, then a single color weft is used for the solid side and several colors of weft for the patterned side on alternating picks.

6-26. Ruana from Bogota, Colombia. Reversible double weave in brushed mohair yarns. Model, Cynthia Davidson.

115

6-28. Woven pleats.

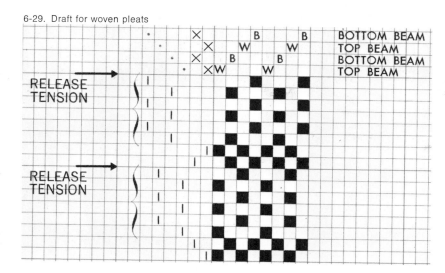

6-29. Draft for woven pleats

DOUBLE WEAVE WITH TWO WARP BEAMS

When the top and bottom layers of a double weave are wound on individual warp beams, the tension of the two layers can be controlled separately and several interesting effects can be obtained. Among these are pleats or woven ribs and fringes.

For pleats or ribs, the procedure is as follows:

(1) Weave just the top layer until twice the desired depth of the pleat is reached. Then release the tension of the top wrap beam and move the beater forward firmly.

(2) Weave both layers of warp together for several picks until the pleat is safely anchored.

For changes in color, the bottom layer can be brought up to be the top layer next time in the same way. Even when only one shuttle is used, the colors change if the warp threads for each layer are different colors.

For fringes you will need several pick-up sticks as long as the width of the warp and as wide as the desired length of the fringe. The procedure is as follows:

(1) Weave several inches of plain weave.

(2) Raise the top layer and insert a pick-up stick under it. Release tension on the top warp beam.

(3) Pull the beater forward, leaving the stick in the warp. Hold the stick tightly and move the beater back to rest position.

(4) Interweave the two layers with several picks of plain weave.

(5) Raise the bottom layer and insert pick-up stick. Release tension on the bottom warp beam.

(6) Repeat steps 3 and 4.

(7) Repeat the entire process several times; then pull the sticks out to use them again as the weaving progresses.

(8) When finished, the loops left by the sticks can be left or cut into fringe.

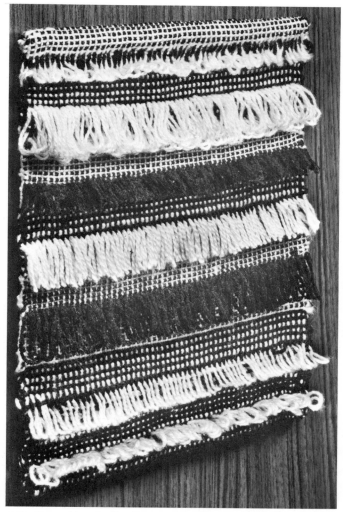

6-30. Woven fringe by Else Regensteiner. (Photo: John W. Rosenthal)

7

DESIGN

Designing for weaving means composing shapes, colors, textures, forms, and space into a harmonious structure. The weaver must not only understand the mechanics of the loom and the techniques of weave construction but must also judge what arrangement of visual elements will best express his intentions and interpret his vision. Designing for weaving is like designing for any visual medium—only the primary materials of expression are fibers, weaves, and the loom rather than paints, brushes, and canvas, or clay and wheel, or metal and hammer.

Many artists apply the "rules" of design instinctively and naturally. However, not only the artist's senses and intuition but also his reason and intellect are needed to transform his ideas into a successful work of art. To understand the principles of composing the elements of design can only help him to approach a problem with competence and assurance. It may make the difference between a significant and a superficial design. But the rules should never obstruct the vision of the artist. They are flexible and changing: they have been reviewed, absorbed, discarded, and broken in every epoch of art according to the individual needs of the artist and the age. They are, and should always be treated as, a helping device, never a limitation. Designing, it must always be remembered, is a most personal vocation, and in the course of time every artist will arrive at his own individual mode of expression.

Designing for weaving requires not only skillful craftsmanship and composition but also an understanding of how to fit these to the functional needs of each project. All fabrics planned and woven for a specific purpose

have their own inherent demands. Drapery fabric must drape but not sag, let in or keep out light, resist fading, and enhance a room. Rugs and upholstery fabric must be strong enough to resist abrasion and hard wear. There is hardly a weaver who does not look forward to designing and weaving a dress or suit fabric, but these materials present numerous questions of function. The purpose and weight of clothing fabric go hand in hand, and the temptation to make material too heavy or bulky is sometimes overwhelming, especially when rich yarns such as tweeds are chosen. But the designer must keep in mind the function of the fabric: is it for summer or winter, formal wear or informal wear, a scarf or an overcoat?

Probably the finest garments ever made were those woven by the "Chosen Women" of the Incas. These women were specially selected and trained to spend their lives spinning and weaving. Using the fiber of the rare vicuña, they made textiles of exceptional beauty. The contemporary weaver cannot devote the same concentration to his work as the pre-Columbian, but the weaving of a beautiful garment, rug, tapestry, or wall hanging is still within easy reach.

The designer's goal is to blend considerations of function with those of form, and these factors are inseparable. What fibers can be used in a particular piece? What setting in the reed? What weave or pattern? Is an open, lacy structure or a close, solid weave most appropriate? Should the design be a repeat or variations on a theme or freely varied? Hand in hand with form and function goes selection of technique. Pattern weaves and basic weaves are particularly suited

Fig. 7-12, enlarged

7-1. "Voie Lactée," ("The Milky Way") by Jean Lurçat. Tapestry woven in black, white, blues, yellows, greens, and reds. (Private collection)

7-2. "Window Hanging," transparent panel by Loraine Gonzalez.

7-3. "Linen Lattice," drapery panel by Julia McVicker and Else Regensteiner. (Photo: John W. Rosenthal)

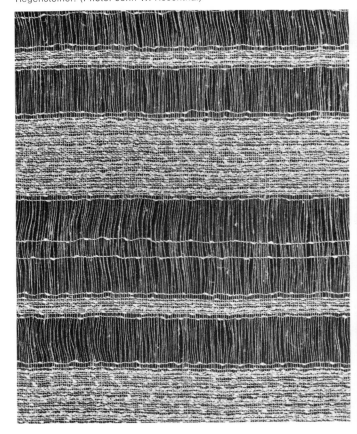

7-4. Pillows and bedspread woven in Summer and Winter variations by Libby Crawford. (Photo: Associated Artists Advertising Agency)

Below:
7-5. Co-ordinated upholstery fabrics by Julia McVicker and Else Regensteiner. Warp of sea island twine, weft of heavy rug wool.

to the large proportions of drapery panels. Two-dimensional designs may be most successfully interpreted in tapestry, where hard and flat edges can be emphasized; for softened and blurred outlines, a pile weave is the best choice.

Whatever the decision, a design must have visual interest yet it must also be a unified and harmonious composition. Shapes may be round, oval, rectangular, square, convex, or concave; they may be realistic or abstract. They may be repeated in an allover pattern or at regular or irregular intervals; they may be varied in size, texture, or color. But the relationship of each form to other forms and to the whole is of utmost importance. When a surface is divided into different parts, the resulting whole can be pleasant or unpleasant, tedious or fascinating. The proportions, the interplay of figure and ground, positive space and negative space, must be planned so that a pleasing balance is achieved.

Texture, of course, is a major visual element in weaving. The designer's goal is to integrate texture with the other elements of the design but to avoid the danger of letting texture overpower or obstruct them.

The laws of nature may well be the laws of art. Proportions in design based on natural proportions will always be pleasing. Definite relationships between the whole and the parts are invariably demonstrated in plant and animal forms. In any good design a focal point of interest

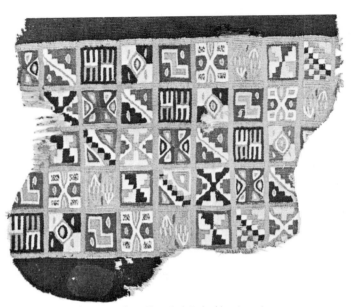

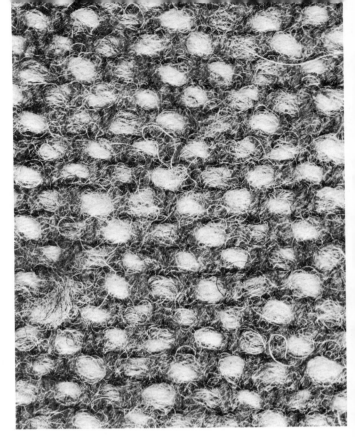

7-6. Fragment of garment from Peru in interlocking tapestry. (Photo courtesy The Art Institute of Chicago)

7-8. Upholstery fabric in wool, mohair, and silk yarns by Julia McVicker and Else Regensteiner.

Coat fabric in broken twill by a student.

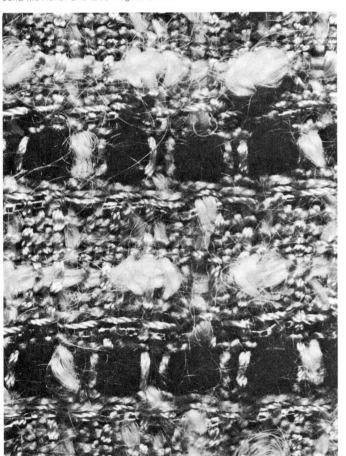

must be present, whether it be a shape, color, or texture. Without one or the other setting the theme, a piece may become boring and insignificant.

All pieces, no matter what their purpose and no matter what their size or scope, must be entities. Top, bottom, beginning, ending, edges—all must be treated as visible parts of the design. Thus, the selection of a rod from which to suspend a wall hanging and the final effort in knotting a fringe to complete a rug, as much as yarns and weaves, are deciding factors in creating a work of artistic value.

Color in weaving is clearly crucial, yet it is the factor about which many weavers feel most uncertain. When they encounter various theories of color, which are certainly valid studies in themselves, they are often bewildered and apt to lose confidence in their own judgment. Reaction to color is extremely personal, however: what to one person is beautiful is, to another, just the opposite. Concepts of color—and tastes—change constantly, as is especially obvious in fashion trends. These changes can also be seen in the use of color in paintings: compare, for instance, the old masters and contemporary works such as those of the color-field painters.

Colors have always been symbolic and expressive, and they were even magical in some cultures. We still associate certain colors with a variety of meanings, feelings, and occasions, yet in this age of space travel, rapid acceleration, and constant motion, color has

7-9. Coat fabric in plaid twill by Lurene Stone.

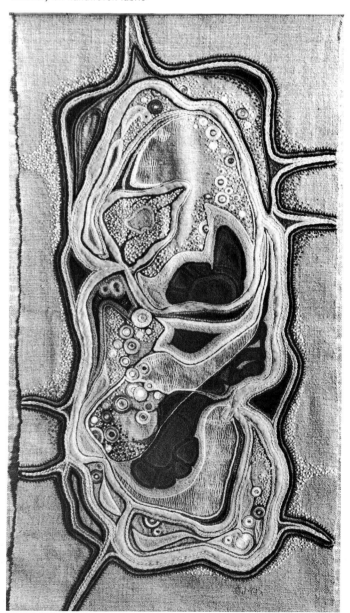

7-10. "Tehilah," wall hanging by Lois G. McBride. Stitchery on handwoven fabric

been freed from convention. Sharp, bright, pure colors are used for sheer delight in their vitality.

The weaver will always choose colors that fit his own mood, purpose, and taste, but it is important to remember that colors act in certain ways of which the weaver must be aware. They never stand alone: they are seen in their surroundings, against backgrounds and neighboring colors. Size, shape, and texture influence color, as do light and shade. Every weaver should possess a color wheel, not just to learn a theory but to gain an understanding of an intricate subject.

Complementary colors placed next to each other—in stripes, for example—intensify each other. But when they are mixed together, as in warp and weft, they may cancel each other out and produce a dirty-looking gray. White and black often have an unexpected effect on imagined color schemes. Weavers are often surprised that a white warp, visualized as neutral, will turn bright weft colors into washed-out tints, while a black warp will bring out the sparkle of strong hues. The highest intensity of color is achieved when warp and weft are the same or closely related in color; monochromatic compositions are extremely subtle.

Fascinating color phenomena occur when colors are juxtaposed. When bright and dull colors are used together, the dull color will seem duller than it really is, the bright color brighter. Strong complementary colors used in equal proportions will cause optical vibration. The same color looks different on two different back-

"Old Women of Arles," painting by Paul Gauguin. (Courtesy of The Art Institute of Chicago)

Experimental twill weaving inspired by "Old Women of Arles," by Joanna Kiljanska.

Color study by Michi Ouchi. The weft thread changes color as it interlocks with other colors in the warp.

Weaving inspired by a turquoise-colored rock, by Else Regensteiner. Plain weave with groups of tied warp threads. The warp is mohair, wool, and silk; the weft, mohair loop yarn and four-ply wool crocheted into a chain.
(Photo: John W. Rosenthal)

7-11. Applique on handwoven wool fabric from Bolivia.

7-12. "Les Trois Grâces," wall hanging by Jay Hinz.

grounds: orange on yellow will appear red; the same orange on red will appear tan. The background tends to absorb its own color, leaving the other component more visible.

The study of color is rich, rewarding, and essential to the weaver. The best recommendation I can make to my readers is to study the color work of painters and other artists, of theorists, and of nature. You will find that there are no ugly colors; there are only pleasant and unpleasant sensations for the viewer, and the skillful weaver will use both sense and sensibility to make the best choice.

The designers of the wall hangings illustrated in Figures 7-12 and 7-13 made this statement about their work: "In our designs the size is the primary consideration; the next concern is to organize the space into a pleasing balance of shape, color, value, and texture. This is as necessary when designing nonobjectively as it is when subject matter is introduced, as was the case in both hangings illustrated—'Owl Study' and 'Les Trois Grâces.' The use of line was introduced to enhance the shapes and emphasize the subject matter."

7-14. "The Crucifixion," three-dimensional hanging by Theo Moorman. (Photo courtesy of the artist)

7-15. Detail of scroll mantle by Ethel Kaplan.

The beautiful pieces in Figures 7-14 and 7-15 are examples of how the weaver combines the particular demands of the project with artistic expression to create a work of art. In one, the weaver made a semi-abstract interpretation of a great theme. Another contemporary weaver, Ethel Kaplan, was confronted by a similar task when she was asked to weave scroll mantles for the Holy Scriptures. She says, of the project, "Scroll mantles must be both decorative and durable, for they are 'dressed' and 'undressed' at least twice a week, being handled by a different person each time. Therefore I used materials which are strong and wear well, but have a graceful, flowing quality when handled. The tiny gold bells, handmade in India, were sewn onto each section and lend a beautiful sound which accompanies the putting on and taking off of the mantles. Inspiration for the colors, bells, and yarn was taken from passages of the Bible. This made the project all the more exciting and interesting to do."

Commissions such as these are a great inspiration for the weaver. They set a definite task and demand the skill of the craftsman together with the sensitivity

7-16. Sea shell.

of the artist. Often, the requirements of an exacting project challenge the weaver to gain a broad understanding of related fields and adapt his work to a fresh context.

Every weaving project, whether it is a simple piece for experiment and exploration or a piece with a specific purpose, is a challenge to the weaver's ingenuity and creative ability. Where does he find the stimulus to imagination that makes each design solution fresh and exciting? The answer is: Everywhere.

Yarns themselves are inspirational. There is hardly an imaginative weaver who will not have a hundred ideas come to him from looking at an array of beautiful yarns or sample cards. Today, with so many exciting threads in every imaginable color and texture on the market, the difficulty usually lies only in making a selection, and in this *In der Beschraenkung zeigt sich erst der Meister*—"limitation really shows the master" (Goethe).

Source material is all around us—we must only learn to see. "You do not see with the lens of the eye. You see through that and by means of that, but you see with the soul of the eye," wrote John Ruskin. Perfect form,

7-17, 7-18. Fabrics inspired by a sea shell, by Sue Zinngrabe.

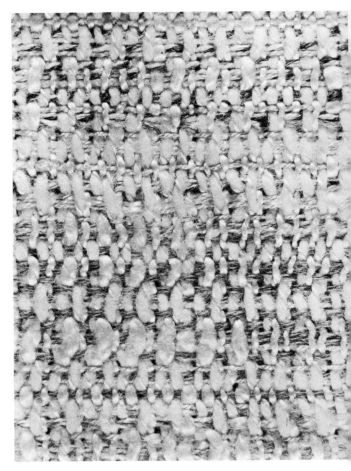

128

perfect proportion, perfect rhythm, perfect color surrounds us, if we will only pay attention. They are in every tree, every branch, every leaf, in unending variety. The texture of bark is rough, smooth, lined, flaky, shiny, dull; flowers are crimson, scarlet, rosy, as well as red, yellow, blue, and every imaginable hue.

Why are flowers of many colors, shapes, and species together on the lawn or in the flower bed never ugly? What is the mystery behind the spiral of the snail's shell, the flowing lines of the creatures of the sea? Why is function in nature always at the same time beautiful? Every plant, every rock, every grain of sand is interesting, perfect, sculptured—with shape, texture, and decoration so integrated with function that we can only marvel at Nature's achievements.

We have all this at our finger tips—sky, mountains, sea, clouds—every form and color we could want. And we have all this for inspiration if we can transpose what we see by means of our creative abilities. The bewildering array, once we have learned to see, again makes discrimination necessary.

Small objects—shells, leaves, feathers, pebbles—when examined carefully, yield colors, shapes, textures.

7-19. Peacock feather.

7-20, 7-21. Fabric and rug inspired by a peacock feather.

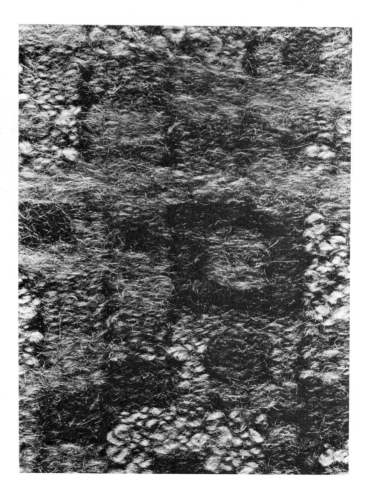

7-22. Zebras.

7-23. Suit fabric derived from zebra pattern by Barbara Meyer.

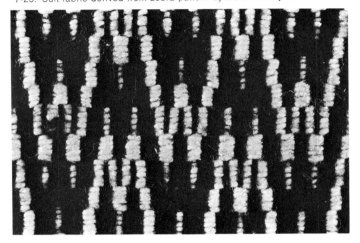

To interpret them in weaving opens the door to new designs.

Landscapes—fields, mountains, lakes, roads, and rivers—are spread out in designs. A thousand rugs and tapestries are there ready for the weaver.

Animals have always played a role in the design of textiles, suggesting never-ending ideas for stripes and spots, blendings of color, and texture. They beckon the weaver with the temptation to wear what the animals do, without depriving the creatures of their coats, their feathers, or their lives.

All the creations of Nature are inspiration, and quick snapshots or sketches will preserve the memory of what is seen until the moment when the right project presents itself, and the image can be brought to the weaver's loom.

And still there is elsewhere to look. Man's own creations are a treasure trove: walking through the city, a variety of architectural forms—doors and windows, pillars and balconies—materials, textures, and proportions present themselves to the perceiving eye. Compositions can be inspired by skyscrapers, and ideas can even spring from a heap of rubble. The forms of tech-

7-24. Inspiration from a bird for three fabrics by Jean Young.

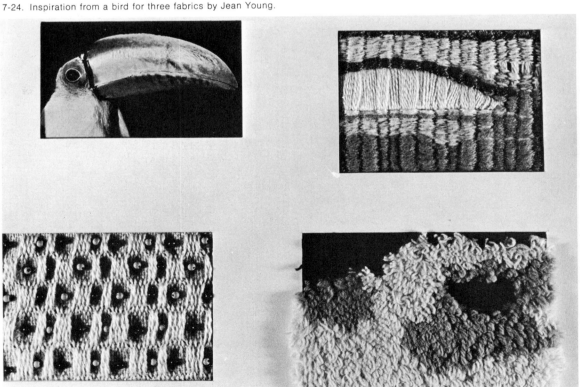

130

7-25. A beautiful fish with many textures and colors.

7-26. Painted warp fabric inspired by the fish, by Oliver Wittasek.

7-27. Another bird inspired these fabrics and a wall hanging by Llubica Stevanov.

7-28. Albrecht Dürer's painting of a hare inspired a brown coat fabric sample by Marsha Ford Anderle.

nology—machines, bridges, highways—are sources, sources as rich as the forms of history. Each small artifact in an exhibition—the work of the pre-Columbian potter, that of the Renaissance sculptor, that of the African wood-carver—can provide encouragement and stimulation.

There is, also, the painter—nobody knows more about art than he. The colors he uses, bright and dull, clashing or harmonious, suggest a world of ideas. Analyze a small section of a painting and you will be surprised at the many colors it contains. Several small sections can be developed in a fabric, and even complete impressions may be interpreted in weaving. If an original painting is not available, a reproduction can help to revive the memory of colors and shapes. In no way is this advice meant to be an encouragement to copy. Imitation can only stifle and obstruct—it can never help the potential artist. Ideas and impressions must be absorbed and assimilated before they can be expressed in a fresh and personal way. But to see and recognize the wealth of designs that surround us in every object, natural and man-made, means the development of the particular ability of the creative artist and weaver.

7-29. Feather poncho from Peru, Tiahuanaco period. (Photo courtesy of The Art Institute of Chicago)

Above right:
7-30. Feather wall plaque inspired by Peruvian feather poncho, by Linda Howard.

Right:
7-31. Fur wall hanging also inspired by Peruvian feather poncho, by Jon Riis.

133

8

TAPESTRY

The term "tapestry" in its true traditional sense refers to a fabric in which the weft yarns cover the warp completely, so the weft colors alone form the design. Characteristically, tapestry is built up with many small areas of color within which the weft yarns travel back and forth. Only in rare instances, when stripes or checkerboard patterns are desired, does the weft traverse the full width of the warp. Instead of shuttles, small finger-wound skeins called butterflies or individual bobbins are used to insert the various colors.

Tapestry is plain weave, although in a few cases twill weave is used. Sometimes other structures are mistakenly called tapestry. Embroidery, which is applied to a previously woven cloth, is not tapestry, nor is painted or printed fabric.

Tapestry weaving is an ancient art. Fragments of tapestries dating from as early as 1483 B.C. have been found in Egyptian tombs. Examples of Coptic weaving from the sixth and seventh centuries A.D. can be found in nearly all the great museums of the world. By seemingly independent development, tapestry weaves were also made in the Americas at the same time. Tapestries from these early periods are a great inspiration for the contemporary weaver. Because each was designed and woven by the same person, they possess great unity of form, material, and concept, and the ancient two-dimensional presentation of design is much in accord with contemporary feelings about art.

It was not until the Middle Ages that tapestry became a mural art. From the late fourteenth to the mid-sixteenth centuries, the art of tapestry weaving flowered in France. The tapestries were made to cover the cold bare walls of castles and churches, and were used as dividers in doorways and halls. They were taken along during wars and hung up between battles wherever camp was established. Commissioned by kings, princes, and great churchmen, they were designed and woven in ateliers in Angers, Paris, and Arras.

Not the weavers themselves but famous painters designed these hangings. They made full-scale paintings called cartoons, which highly skilled artisan-weavers faithfully copied. These tapestries always told a story: they interpreted myths, related scenes from feudal life —the hunts and the wars—and depicted tales from the Bible, allegories, fantasies, and legends.

The most beautiful of these masterpieces, perhaps, are the famous "Apocalypse" series at the Chateau D'Angers, the "Lady with the Unicorn" now at the Cluny Museum in Paris, and the "Hunt of the Unicorn," a series of *mille-fleurs* ("thousand flowers," from the design of the background) tapestries now in the Cloisters Collection of the Metropolitan Museum of Art in New York.

In contrast to these delightful works, French tapestries woven in the great studios of the Gobelin and at Aubusson from the seventeenth century onward were conceived by painters who had little understanding of the weaving medium and insisted on exact imitations of their paintings. Instead of the relatively limited color range of medieval designs, their palettes included from four hundred to seven hundred shades. The tapestries were hardly distinguishable from the paintings and were copied over and over again. The great art of tapestry weaving deteriorated and was nearly lost.

8-1. Peruvian slit tapestry of cotton and wool, 1000-1500 A.D. (Photo courtesy of The Art Institute of Chicago)

8-2. Tapestry by Jean Lurçat. Woven in Aubusson in shades of blue, orange, yellow, and black, it depicts a charming underwater scene. (Private collection)

8-3. "Pavane," tapestry by Robert Wogenscky. Shades of yellow, orange, brown, white, and black. (Private collection)

For its revival, we have to thank a group of young French painters. The foremost of these was Jean Lurçat who, long fascinated by the potentials of tapestry art, studied its techniques and gained a true understanding of the intrinsic qualities of the craft. Lurçat realized that a design had to be conceived for the medium of weaving, not for that of painting. He used a limited palette, but with only twenty pure shades placed skillfully side by side, he achieved effects in which the textural quality of weaving was enhanced instead of ignored. The subject matter of his tapestries, like that of the Middle Ages, is nature, allegories, and fantasies, and his work has dramatic mural dimensions. Well-known artists such as Marcel Gromaire, Jean Picard Le Doux, Dom Robert, Raoul Dufy, and Robert Wogenscky followed his example. The renaissance of tapestry weaving had begun.

Today tapestries are used once more in great public buildings and in homes. They have an affinity with architecture, and their color and warmth make them especially suitable to large modern expanses of stone, glass, and steel. And in tapestry may be found a blending of artistic freedom and the discipline of true craftsmanship.

8-4. "The World Is Shimmering," tapestry by Josefina Robirosa. The yarns are natural and vegetable-dyed in many shades of red, orange, green, and yellow. (Photo: John W. Rosenthal)

8-5. Tapestry in the making on a contemporary vertical loom.

8-6. Tapestry being woven on a horizontal loom in Ecuador.

"The World is Shimmering" (Figure 8-4) is a contemporary tapestry by a young painter, Josefina Robirosa, from Buenos Aires, Argentina, and was woven by Indians high in the Andes Mountains. M. Larochette, a designer-weaver who was trained in Aubusson and who started the Indian workshop, chose the little village of Bariloche because its pure water from the mountains would not affect the wool's color and texture, and because the Indian women there seemed to have a particular aptitude for weaving. Miss Robirosa says: "I have always loved tapestry. It is very noble and very warm, very different from oil painting. It takes about fifteen days to make a design. I generally make a small one. Then I photograph it and project it to the size it will actually be on the wall. I trace the design on a piece of paper. Sometimes I invent directly in actual size. I number the colors—there are 150 altogether—for the women. It takes two women working together to weave it. When the tapestry comes back, I know who did it. I already know their hands by name."

Even if no large ambitious project is planned, every weaver should at least make a sample to explore tapestry weaving, which is basically very simple. There are two traditional techniques: the high-warp (haute-

lisse) method using the vertical upright loom (the technique of the Gobelin factories), and the low-warp (basse-lisse) using the horizontal foot loom (the Aubusson technique). Actually, any loom on which a plain weave structure can be woven may be used. The upright two-harness loom is, for the modern handweaver, the most convenient, because both sides of the tapestry can be observed during the weaving. On a two-harness loom the threads are alternated; a straight threading may be used on a four-harness loom.

Carpet warp, cotton threads, or rug linen can be used. The warp should be strong, and can be doubled both through heddles and reed. The number of warp threads per inch depends on the size of the weft threads. Because the weft must cover the warp completely, the spaces between the warp threads must be wider than the width of the weft threads used. For a sample to be made with a four-ply wool weft, five warp threads per inch are recommended, with two extra threads for each selvage.

Weft yarns may be wool, cotton, silk, or synthetic. It is advisable to use a smooth, soft weft, which will beat down easily; it should never be a slippery yarn. Most frequently, tapestries are made with wool wefts.

8-7, 8-8. The design of the tapestry being woven has been traced on the warp. The weaving proceeds from bottom to top, and the back side faces the weaver.

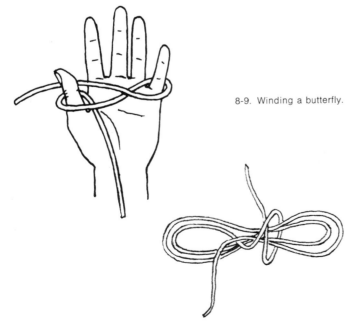

8-9. Winding a butterfly.

Traditionally, tapestries are woven sideways. Not only is it easier to weave lines horizontally than vertically, but the weft threads are the closer and sturdier part of the tapestry. The cartoon is laid under the warp threads to guide the weaver, and the outline of the design is marked directly on the warp threads. When the tapestry is finished, the warp threads run horizontally from selvage to selvage, and it is hung by the weft. Also, traditionally, tapestry is woven with the back side facing the weaver. But contemporary weavers do not always follow traditional methods. Individual craftsmen develop their own style, and very often their work can be recognized. Rules are not strict any more. Tapestries frequently are woven from bottom to top with the right side facing the weaver; in many cases the design is developed directly on the loom without a cartoon, and, as with the ancient tapestries, the weaver and designer are often the same person.

When weaving from selvage to selvage, a variety of effects can be obtained by simple color changes. For horizontal lines, alternate several lines of one color with several lines of another color. For vertical lines, alternate two lines of color, and for checkerboard, change the rotation of alternative lines of color by weaving two picks of the same color at the desired changing points. Designs can also be made by shaping or molding the weft threads as they are woven into the warp.

In a true tapestry, however, the shuttle does not travel from selvage to selvage. The weft is wound in individual butterflies (Figure 8-9) as needed, and the design is composed of many individual areas. With the background knowledge of a few simple techniques, the weaver can create many varied designs.

SLIT METHOD

(1) Open the shed. Bring the two colored wefts from opposite directions through the shed to the meeting point and to the surface of the warp.

(2) Change shed. Insert both weft yarns again into shed, using adjacent warp threads to turn back to their area of design. Where the two colors meet, an opening is left between the adjacent warp threads (Figure 8-11). This opening becomes a slit as the weaving continues.

The clean-cut line that this method produces may be used as part of the weave, or as decoration. If the slits become too long or are unwanted, they can be sewn together afterwards.

If the threads meet in regular progression at consecutive warp threads, diagonal slits will be produced (Figure 8-12). Diagonals can move gradually to the right or to the left and produce only small openings (Figure 8-13).

8-10. Tapestry made by slit method by Cynthia Lubliner. Rust and natural wool.

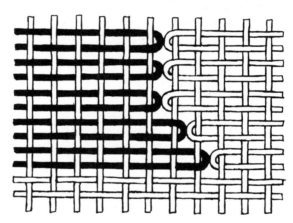

8-12. Straight and diagonal slits.

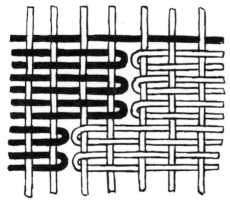

8-11. Straight slits.

8-13. Small slits.

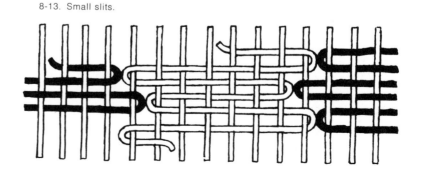

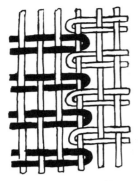

8-14. Weft interlocking over common warp thread.

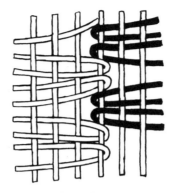

8-16. Dovetailing.

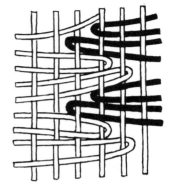

8-17. Irregular dovetailing.

8-15. Interlocking weft threads.

INTERLOCKING OVER COMMON WARP THREADS

In this method, wefts of different colors are carried around a common warp thread. In alternating sheds weave two picks back and forth, first one, then the other color, using the same warp thread for their return (Figure 8-14). The edges in this joining are not clearly defined, but produce feathery or saw-tooth interlocking effects.

INTERLOCKING WEFT THREADS

Wefts of different colors may interlock with each other between warp threads, then return in the alternating shed, to their own side (Figure 8-15).

DOVETAILING

Several wefts of one design run back and forth in alternating sheds, first on one side, then on the other side. The same or a different warp thread may be used for their interlocking (Figures 8-16 and 8-17).

HATCHING

Two weft threads run back and forth in alternating sheds (Figure 8-18). This creates feathery lines in areas of solid color.

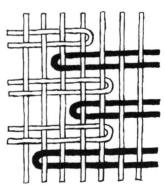

8-18. Hatching.

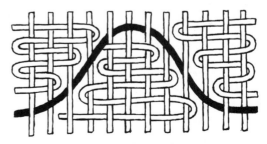

8-19. Molding and outlining a shape with a contrasting thread.

MOLDING AND SHAPING

Background threads forming a triangular shape may be built up and molded with the fingers to push the threads higher or lower in the design. Threads of contrasting color may be used to outline and emphasize these shapes (Figure 8-19).

COMBINED TECHNIQUES

Some contemporary tapestries are not completely weft-faced, but combine interlocking weave and ordinary plain weave or twill, with warp and weft threads showing in equal amounts. The warp may be left completely unwoven in sections as an organic part of the design, or warp threads may be wrapped with yarns singly or in groups to introduce open effects (Figures 8-21 and 8-22). Slits themselves may carry the design, as illustrated in Figures 8-23 and 8-24. Knots, loops, and fringes or other techniques such as soumak (see Chapter 9) also may be incorporated, as in Figure 8-31. Whatever you plan, remember that a simple composition and a sensitive approach to design and the potentials of the medium can turn an exploration of tapestry weaving into a true expression of art.

8-21. Detail of tapestry with partly open weave.

8-20. Tapestry by Napoleon Henderson. Black, natural, and gray wool yarns.

8-22. Tapestry with open weave and wrapped warp threads.

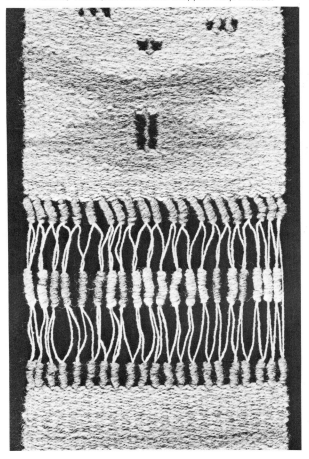

141

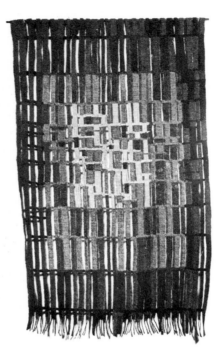

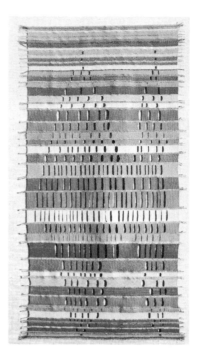

8-24. Room divider made in slit tapestry by Kathryn Ux. (Photo courtesy of Grand Rapids Art Museum)

8-23. Slit tapestry by Jon Riis. Fine mohair yarns on cotton warp.

8-25. "Winter Woods," tapestry by Carol Weston. Wool on cotton rug warp, in earth and wood colors.

8-26. "Masquerade," tapestry by Ulla-May Berggren. (Photo courtesy of Marna Johnson)

8-27. Op-art tapestry by Esther Gotthoffer.
Red, white, and blue wool on blue linen warp.
(Photo: Edith Harper)

8-28. "Coptic Cross," slit tapestry with knotted loops
by Leora K. Stewart.

8-29. "Girl Looking Into Mirror," tapestry
by Nancy Crump.

8-30. "The Two Great Lights," tapestry by Terry
Illes. White, red-violet, and navy wool on cotton
warp. (Photo courtesy of Marna Johnson)

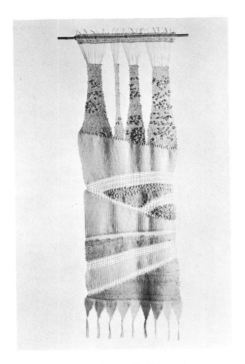

8-31. "Winter Landscape," slit tapestry, soumak, loop pile, leno, and other weaves by Diane Wiersba. Natural silk, wool, and mohair. (Photo: Bob Bender)

8-33. "Egyptian Beads," tapestry by Terry Illes. Orange, yellow, and green on emerald wool warp, with Egyptian beads. (Photo courtesy of Marna Johnson)

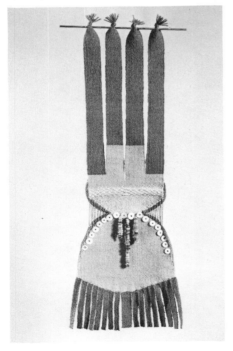

8-32. "Galaxy," tapestry by Esther Gotthoffer. Gold and Blue. (Photo: Lodder)

Tapestries woven in interlocking technique, from Ecuador.

9

RUGS

The handweaver's rugs are usually works of art, not just floor coverings. Their size, material, color, design, and technique of execution must be carefully planned to make them functional as well as beautiful. As in every weaving project, technique is the father of design and needs to be studied first. Only with mastery of the fundamental structures can the weaver make rugs that are both aesthetically and technically perfect.

It is not possible, in the framework of this book, to exhaust all the methods of rug weaving. The techniques described here, however, are meant to provide the weaver with the working knowledge to plan and execute original designs. Three types of rugs are included: the knotted piles, the woven piles, and flat woven rugs.

A rug loom must be sturdy but need not be complicated. It can consist of an upright frame on which the warp is wound vertically, with a fork or comb as the beater. Contemporary harness looms with foot treadles and beater, whether vertical or horizontal, are very serviceable. For knotted pile and tapestry rugs, only two harnesses are needed; for the others, four or eight harnesses are required.

Warp yarns for rugs must be especially strong and not slippery. Rug linen in sizes 5/10, 8/3, or 8/4 is excellent, and seine cotton or carpet warps in these sizes also make good warps. Since making a rug takes many days and sometimes weeks, its wearing quality should be assured by choosing the best yarns available. Wool has always been the weaver's first choice and has kept this place in spite of the proliferation of synthetic yarns. Swedish rya wools, Persian rug yarns, and other long-fiber wools give luxurious piles and the guarantee of excellent wear. Different sizes and types of wool can be mixed, and mohair, alpaca, silk, or linen can be added to enrich and bring variety to a wool pile.

The tabby yarn may be fine or coarse, but it should also be strong and durable. Cotton may be used, but wool is always preferable. I have found a blend of Swedish cow hair and wool to be an excellent background for rows of pile or fringe. However, this is a heavy yarn and will cover the warp only when the warp is set with six or fewer threads to the inch.

KNOTTED PILE RUGS

Lovers of Oriental carpets and rugs are familiar with one of the most treasured results of the weaver's skill and ingenuity—the hand-knotted pile. This technique is believed to date back as far as 5000 B.C., coming to us from Central Asia, Iran, India, China, and the Caucasus. Fabulous carpets were described in old manuscripts, thus remaining alive even after the originals were lost. The history, description, and classification of various types of rugs, always named after the district or village in which they are produced, make a fascinating study.

Oriental pile rugs have, on the average, between eighty and three hundred knots tied in a square inch. However, 2,400 knots per square inch were counted in the fragment of one Indian prayer rug of the seventeenth century, now in the Altman Collection of The Metropolitan Museum of Art in New York.

The contemporary handweaver cannot possibly match the skill of the Oriental craftsman who can tie as many

9-1. Oriental rug in Ghiordes technique. Nineteenth century.
(Photo courtesy of The Art Institute of Chicago)

tremely close pile of Oriental rugs, only one or two picks are inserted between the rows. In contemporary rugs, the number of tabbies depends on the desired texture, density, and length of the pile and can range from as few as two to as many as twenty-four picks per inch.

It should be noted that it is very important to keep the weft loose when inserting it into the shed for the tabby. "Bubbling," or laying in the weft in an arc instead of pulling it tight, will prevent the rug from drawing in at the edges and narrowing.

At the beginning and again at the end of the rug, several inches of a flat, weft-faced tabby are woven. For the main area, the rug knots are tied, one row at a time, across the width of the warp. After each row is knotted, the background picks are woven: then the next row of knots is tied. The process is repeated until the rug is finished. If fringe is planned, the loose warp threads at the beginning and end of the rug are interknotted after the rug has been taken off the loom.

Rugs should be planned carefully on graph paper, first in a small sketch, then full scale. The scale should be made according to the number of knots per square inch, so that the drawing can be followed row by row on the loom. A color sketch may be made by glueing small pieces of yarn on graph paper, but the detailed drawing is indispensable both for the actual weaving and for working out the amount of yarn needed.

Estimating the right amount of yarn needed for a pile

9-2. Design for a rug by Barbara Fine. In this drawing, one square equals one inch.

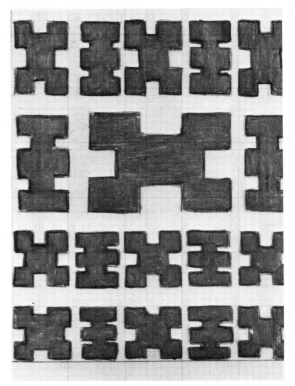

as 10,000 knots each day. Even though Oriental rugs provide the basic technique for knotted piles, it would be disastrous for us to try to copy their style or design. Each weaver must make his own adaptation of the old techniques and methods. Contemporary rugs are, by comparison, coarse in texture and slow in weaving, but they fit into modern surroundings and express the modern weaver's creative world.

The knotted pile rug consists of one warp and two different wefts, one for the pile, the other for the background. The setting of the warp in the reed is farther apart than in ordinary weaving because the warp is to be covered by the two wefts. Six to eight threads per inch have made good rug warps in my experience; the result is three or four knots per inch. Although various other settings can be chosen, depending on the yarn and desired texture and density of pile, the settings given here are based on four knots per inch.

Selvages on both sides must be strengthened (this is true in all rugs), and the last two adjacent dents should therefore be threaded double.

The density of the pile is determined by the number of knots per square inch *and* the number of tabby picks thrown between the rows of knots. In the fine and ex-

rug may seem a puzzling feat of mathematics to the inexperienced weaver. The following guidelines are intended as a starting point; with experience, you will learn to adjust for the yarn selected.

Warp

Eight threads per inch. Multiply the width of the warp (in inches) by eight for the total number of warp threads. Multiply this by the desired length of the warp (in inches) and divide by thirty-six to get the total yardage needed.

Pile

Four knots per inch and two threads per knot, or eight threads per inch. The yarn for each knot must be about two and a half times the desired length of the pile. For a short pile, use three and a half inches of yarn for each knot. Thus, twenty-eight inches of yarn (8 x 3½) are needed per inch. Multiply by the width of the warp (in inches) and the number of rows planned and divide by thirty-six for the total yardage needed.

For a longer pile, use five and three-quarter inches of yarn for each knot, or forty-six inches of yarn per inch.

Tabby

Twenty tabby picks per square inch. For one inch of tabby, one and a quarter inches of yarn are needed; thus, twenty-five inches of yarn (20 x 1¼) are needed per square inch of tabby.

Ghiordes and Senna Knots

There are two knots derived from Oriental rug techniques—the Ghiordes (Turkish) and the Senna (Persian). Of the two, the Ghiordes knot is most widely used today. The tufts of pile yarn come in pairs between two warp threads, leaning slightly toward the weaver.

The yarn for the knots can either be cut into individual lengths or unwound from a small skein or butterfly. Individually tied knots allow the greatest scope for subtle variations and assure absolute control over the smallest areas of design.

To cut yarn in uniform lengths, make a gauge from a wood or metal rod or two pieces of strong cardboard fastened back to back, as illustrated in Figure 9-3. The yarn for each color is wound around the gauge without

9-3. Gauge for cutting uniform lengths of yarn for pile.

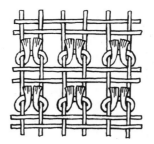

9-4. Ghiordes knots, short pile, with two tabby picks between rows of knots.

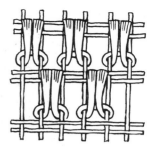

9-5. Ghiordes knots, long pile. In this diagram, the knots are alternated.

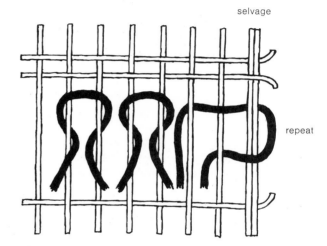

9-6. Yarn woven at the selvage instead of knotted.

overlapping and is sliced along the edge with a knife, razor blade, or scissors. Keep each color separately so the yarn can be used singly or in combinations. Blending several shades of the same color in a single knot gives more depth and brilliance to the pile than if only one hue is used throughout. Not only bright colors but also many natural shades of wool can be beautifully blended, and dark outlines will emphasize a design.

To make the Ghiordes knot, lay a length of cut yarn over two warp threads and pass the ends behind and between them, as shown in Figure 9-4. Two, three, or more strands of yarn can be used in each knot. If a small skein is used, the yarn is cut as the skein is moved from one group of warps to the next. If the color changes, the skeins can be left hanging in the area in which they are used.

The placement of the knots in the warp may be alternated in order to avoid small openings on the back (Figure 9-5). At the selvages the yarn should be woven over and under the two outside threads (Figure 9-6) instead of being tied in a knot between them; this makes a solid, flat edge.

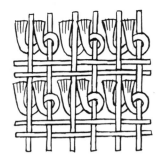

9-7. Senna knots.

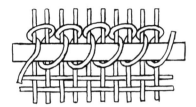

9-8. Knots made over a rod with a continuous ball of yarn.

After the row of knots has been made across the width of the loom according to the design, the shed is opened, the necessary number of tabbies inserted, and the weft beaten down.

To make the Senna knot, one end of the piece of yarn is left outside the two warp threads and the other end is passed under the first thread and over and under the second, ending up between the two threads (Figure 9-7).

As with the Ghiordes knots, the Senna knots may be alternated to avoid openings on the back.

At the selvages the yarn should also be woven over and under the two outside threads. This is not neccessary, however, if a third method of knotting is used. In this case, a continuous ball of yarn is guided between the two warp threads down and to the left, then brought up over them to the right and in between and carried under a rod cut to the desired width (Figure 9-8). When the ball is then inserted between the next group of warp threads, a loop has been formed; it can be cut or left as it is. This method is only desirable, however, when complete rows of the same color are planned or when the pile is to be left in loops.

Rya and Flossa Rugs

The Ghiordes knot is the basis for the Scandinavian techniques, rya and flossa. The difference between a rya rug and a flossa rug lies in the density and length of the pile. Flossa pile is short and close and stands up straight. Only a few picks of tabby are woven between the rows, and fine details of design will show clearly. Flossa rugs resemble Orientals. Rya rugs have a longer and, sometimes, shaggier pile, and there may be as many as twenty picks of tabby between rows of knots.

Actually, there is no rule as to the texture or length of the pile in either kind of rug as long as the background is covered and the pile is full and rich. The surface of both flossa and rya rugs can be designed with various heights of pile, and the knots may be placed in clusters that form designs on a flat tapestry surface. Since fine details are often lost when the pile is long, however, the design areas in rya rugs should be large and bold.

WOVEN PILE RUGS

Since the early nineteenth century, commercial power looms have been used for the weaving of pile carpets. The handweaver can also weave rugs that are not hand-knotted but woven with either warp pile or weft pile on horizontal looms. Although these rugs cannot compete in quality with hand-knotted ones because the pile is not so securely fastened, they can be woven quickly and efficiently. Once the technique of warping and threading for them is understood, weaving proceeds at much the same speed as ordinary shuttle work. The lim-

9-9. Rya rug in handspun wools by Kathryn Ux. (Photo courtesy of Grand Rapids Art Museum)

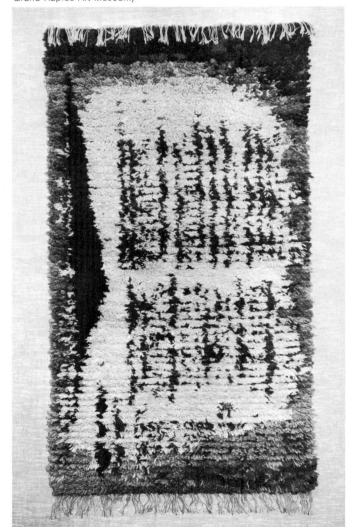

9-10. Rya rug in heavy wool by a student.

9-11. Sculptured rug with pile of various heights designed by Nell Znamierowski for Regal Rugs.

9-12. Sample rug with warp pile woven over a rod by Takeko Nomiya. Part of the pile is cut, part is left in loops. (Photo: John W. Rosenthal)

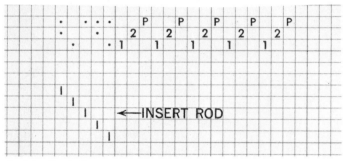

Draft for Fig. 9-12

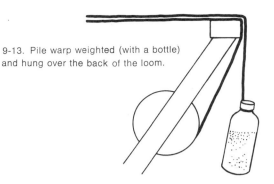

9-13. Pile warp weighted (with a bottle) and hung over the back of the loom.

To make this weave, 5/3 rug wool or cotton warp, sixteen threads per inch, is rolled on to the bottom warp beam for the background. Swedish rya wool, eight threads per inch, is rolled on to the top beam or left hanging over the back for the pile. The yarn for the pile must be approximately three times the length of the background warp, depending on the thickness of the pile yarn. You will also need five rods made of wood or metal for pulling up the pile. The rods should be as long as the width of the loom; their diameter depends on the desired size of the pile. Flat sticks may be used instead.

The threading of the heddles is:

harnesses 1 and 2 — background thread
harness 3 — pile thread

The reed used is eight dents per inch, with two background threads and one pile thread sleyed through the same dent.

The treadling sequence is:

1-3 (background)
2-3 (background)
3 (raise harness, insert rod, and release tension on top warp beam)
1 (background)
2-3 (background)

This sequence is then repeated from the beginning. If the pile yarn is very thick, the background picks may be repeated before the pile is raised. The rods are left in the pile until the fifth one has been inserted; then the first rod is removed and used again, thus rotating the rods continuously to make the pile. Note that the tension of the pile warp may be adjusted as necessary, but it must always be released when a rod is inserted.

The pile may be cut during the course of weaving or it may be left in loops.

Four-Harness Double-Corduroy Weave

The double-corduroy weave, as developed by the well-known weaver Peter Collingwood, was first introduced to handweavers in his workshops. The technique was first published in *Shuttle Craft* by Harriet Tidball and then presented in extended form in Mr. Collingwood's indispensable book, *The Techniques of Rug Weaving*. It is with the permission of both authors that Mr. Collingwood's directions are given here.

itations imposed by loom control are a challenge for the designer, and two distinctive loom-controlled systems are excellent additions to the handweaver's vocabulary. These are three-harness pile weave (pile rugs made by an extra warp) and four-harness double-corduroy weave (pile rugs made by an extra weft).

Three-Harness Pile Weave

The three-harness pile weave is intriguing because of the simplicity and speed with which beautiful thick pile rugs can be woven. The sample shown in Figure 9-12 was made on a horizontal loom with three harnesses and two warp beams (if two beams are not available, the pile warp can hang free over the back of the loom with weights attached, as illustrated in Figure 9-13).

In double corduroy, the pile weft alternately weaves and floats for equal distances across the warp, and the pile is created by cutting the floats. The technique is based on overshot blocks of five threads. There are twenty threads in a repeat, five on each harness. The warp must contain either a complete repeat or a complete repeat and a half—if the repeat is split in any other way, the weave will not be successful. The length of the pile in the double corduroy is controlled by pulling up the floats across the loom as each row is woven. For a short pile very little has to be pulled up because the pile is half the length of the float. For a longer pile, start to pull up the floats by hand from the side of the selvage that the shuttle has just left.

Cotton or linen rug warp in sizes 8/3, 8/4, or 6/10 is suitable for the weave. Use six warp ends per inch for a close pile, four for a looser, shaggier pile.

Two weft yarns are required: a ground weft that never appears in the pile and makes a plain weave throughout, and a pile weft (or wefts). The ground weft can be a six-ply rug wool or blend of cow hair and wool; six-ply rug wool (for a close setting of the warp) or nine-ply (when the warp is set wider apart) or other combinations of yarns can be used for the pile weft.

The threading (from the left side to the right on the front of the loom) is:

4,1,4,1,4
3,4,3,4,3
2,3,2,3,2
1,2,1,2,1

9-14. Double-corduroy rug with cut and uncut pile by Gwynne Lott.

Repeat these units as often as needed across the warp. For the last two dents, at the selvages, use two threads through both heddles and reed.

There are six picks. Two are plain weave for the ground weft, the other four are for the pile weft, and each consists of raising a single harness. The wefts must be thrown into the sheds in a predetermined order that depends on whether complete repeats are being used or the threading ends with a half of the repeat.

With a whole number of repeats, harness 1 gives a pile shed with a warp group raised at both edges; harness 3 gives a pile shed that has no warp group raised at either selvage; harness 2 gives a warp group raised at the right selvage only; and harness 4 gives a pile shed with a warp group raised at the left selvage only. With a whole number and a half, harness 1 raises a warp group at the right selvage but none at the left; harness 3 raises a warp group at the left selvage only; harness 2 raises warp groups at both edges; and harnes 4 does not raise a warp group at either edge. This creates the intricacy of the weave, which is characterized by selvages with no pile protruding.

It is very important to follow the correct sequence of inserting the shuttle on either the right- or left-hand side of the warp. The procedure for weaving with a *whole number of repeats* on the loom is as follows:

(1) Raise harnesses 1 and 3 and weave ground weft from left to right.

(2) Raise harness 1 and weave pile weft from left to right; pull up floats to desired height of pile. (When beginning a rug, leave the end of the weft hanging out in the first space between raised warps. At the beginning and end of the rug, take a separate piece of weft half the normal thickness, loop it around the selvage thread, and put it in the shed, meeting the beginning of the pile in the first space.) Cut the weft about four inches from the right selvage.

(3) Raise harness 3 and weave pile weft from right to left. This is the shed that reaches neither selvage, so leave a tail of weft protruding from the extreme right raised warp group and cut the weft about two inches beyond the point where it emerges from the warp group on the extreme left.

(4) Raise harnesses 2 and 4 and weave ground weft from right to left.

(5) Raise harness 2. Tuck in the pile weft (cut after raising harness 1) under the first group at the right. Weave pile weft from left to right, leaving a tail of it protruding from the warp group at the extreme left. Cut the weft in the space between the warp groups nearest the right selvage.

(6) Raise harness 4 and weave pile weft from right to left. Leave a tail of it protruding from the warp group on the extreme right. Do not cut the weft.

This completes a sequence. The shuttle is now at the left selvage, to be thrown when harness is raised to weave the first pile weft of the sequence again.

The procedure for weaving with threading that ends *with a half of a repeat* is as follows:

(1) Raise harnesses 2 and 4 and weave ground weft from left to right.

(2) Raise harness 2 and weave pile weft from left to right. Start at selvage as described in step 2 above for beginning of rug only. Cut weft at right selvage.

(3) Raise harness 4 and weave pile weft from right to left. Cut beyond warp group at the extreme left. This shed has no warp group reaching the selvage.

(4) Raise harnesses 1 and 3 and weave ground weft from right to left.

(5) Raise harness 1. Tuck in the weft cut when harness 2 was raised. Weave pile weft from left to right and cut it in the space between the warp groups nearest the right selvage.

(6) Raise harness 3 and weave pile weft from right to left, leaving a tail of it protruding at the right selvage. Do not cut the weft.

This sequence is then repeated.

With scissors or a razor blade, cut the pile in vertical columns of floats when two or three inches have been woven. (Peter Collingwood uses a small wire loop, shown in Figure 9-15, to pull up the floats for cutting them.)

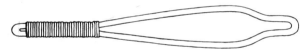

9-15. Wire loop for pulling up corduroy pile, designed by Peter Collingwood.

Peter Collingwood has also invented an ingenious method of cutting the pile in different lengths, which he calls "double cutting." He inserts his wire loop under two adjacent horizontal columns. In this position, the loop cannot move from side to side, and when the two columns of floats are cut simultaneously, one gives a long, the other a short pile. Many different effects can be produced by this off-center cutting of the float; one example is shown in Figure 9-16.

The rug pictured in Figure 9-17 was also woven in double corduroy, but the design was created by inlaying the pile weft. In order to get the very acutely angled shapes, the rug was made in two strips with the warp running horizontally, as shown in the diagram.

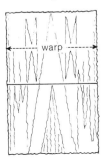

9-16. Double-corduroy rug by Peter Collingwood. The design was produced by "double cutting" some of the pile. (Photo: Charles Seely, courtesy of the artist)

9-17. Double-corduroy rug by Peter Collingwood. (Victoria and Albert Museum, London. Photo: Charles Seely, courtesy of the artist) The structure of the rug is shown in the diagram.

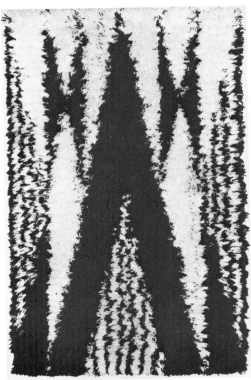

9-18. Kilim rug from Asia Minor. Nineteenth century. (Textile Museum, Washington, D.C. Photo: O. L. Varela)

9-19. Soumak rug, detail.

FLAT WOVEN RUGS

Flat rugs have no pile: the surface is formed by one weft that completely covers the warp. Some flat rugs (the tapestry and soumak weaves) are finger-controlled; others (the bound weave and stuffer rugs) are loom-controlled. Both kinds offer wide scope for design and make easy, valuable projects for experimentation.

Tapestry Rugs

There are two kinds of tapestry rugs: the Kilim, usually associated with the slit technique, and the interlocking tapestry rug, exemplified by Navajo weaving such as the rug in Figure 9-20.

The basic structure of tapestry rugs is plain weave. Oriental Kilims are woven with thin but strong wool yarns and are, because of their slit construction, more suitable for covers and hangings than for floor coverings. The spacing of the warp threads depends on the size of the weft, and as in the case of contemporary tapestry, fewer warp threads are used than in the true Orientals.

Although not so delicate as the Kilims, the interlocking tapestry weave used in American Indian rugs never-

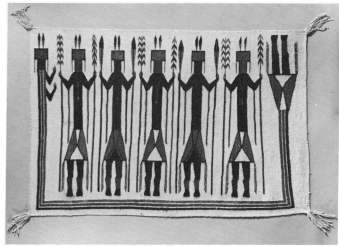

9-20. Navajo rug from Shiprock area, Arizona. Handspun wool in browns, blues, turquoise, and red on a white ground. (Photo: John W. Rosenthal)

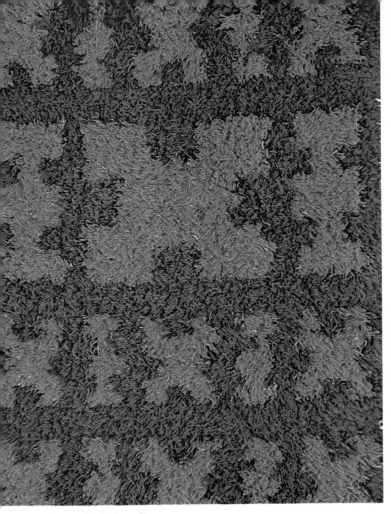

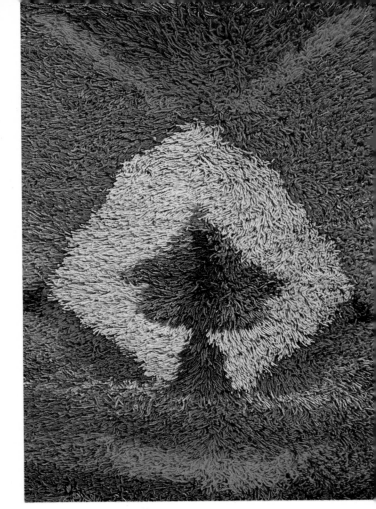

Rya rug by Barbara Fine.

Detail of rya rug by Molly Simons.

Detail of rya rug by Barbara Fine.

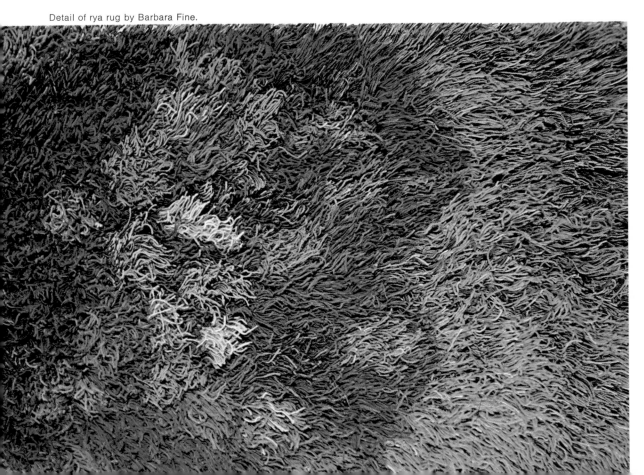

9-21, 9-22. Soumak hanging by Marci Riedel and detail showing herringbone effect of the weave. Red, blue, black, and natural wool on cotton warp. Because the yarns are soft and the weave is somewhat elastic, the piece is better used as a hanging than as a rug.

theless has a special beauty that derives from the simplicity and strength of the Indian designs and their unusual and excellent craftsmanship. Instead of the hard twisted fine wool of the Kilims, the Indian rugs are made of soft handspun thick yarns that give texture to the surface.

To explore the possibilities of tapestry rugs of both kinds, samples may be made with carpet warp or rug linen in size 10/5, 8/3, or 8/4 set five to eight threads per inch (depending on the weft yarn). Double threads in heddles and reed are recommended for selvages. Any good rug wool or cotton yarn can be used for the weft. Hard-wearing Swedish cow hair and wool mixtures, mohair, or worsted rug yarns are also good choices, and several strands may be used together in the shed.

The techniques of tapestry weaving are described in Chapter 8.

Soumak Rugs

Soumak and Shemakha are two weaving centers in Asia Minor where the technique generally called soumak originated. Soumak has the flat appearance of tapestry weaves, but it is actually closely related to the Ghiordes knot. Woven without making a pile, soumak is a wrapping of weft threads over warp threads. Two different weft yarns are used: a fine one, on a shuttle, for the tabby and a heavier one, in a butterfly, for the soumak. The tabby is hidden by the soumak in the weaving.

The procedure, illustrated in Figure 9-23, is as follows:

(1) Weave several rows of tabby.

(2) Starting on the left side of the warp with the shed closed, let the weft travel over two warp threads to the right and under two warp threads to the left. (Leave an end of the weft yarn hanging out; it can be woven into the rug later.) Then let the weft travel over four threads to the right and under two threads to the left. Continue bringing it over four threads to the right and under two to the left to the end of the warp.

(3) Open shed for tabby A. Throw shuttle carrying the finer yarn across the warp and close the shed.

(4) Return the soumak weft from the right side to the left by letting it travel over two warp threads to the left and under two warp threads to the right, then over four warp threads to the left and under two to the right. Continue bringing it over four threads and under two to the end of the warp.

(5) Open shed for tabby B. Throw shuttle carrying the finer yarn across the warp and close the shed.

(6) Repeat the sequence of soumak and tabbies to the desired length of the rug.

When the soumak is woven alternately from right to left and from left to right, the yarns slant in opposite directions, producing a herringbone or knit effect. To make the threads slant in the same direction throughout, the soumak weft can be cut after each row is fin-

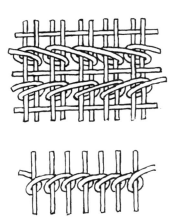

9-23. Soumak technique (top) and soumak woven over one warp thread.

ished and started again from the same side. Other variations include wrapping the weft over only one warp thread, encircling it completely, as illustrated in Figure 9-23. This creates a finer and closer texture. Weft colors can be changed as desired, and the ends may be left hanging on the reverse, as in a tapestry, or may be darned into the weave.

9-24. Bound-weave rug by Takeko Nomiya.
Draft by Astra Strobel for Fig. 9-24

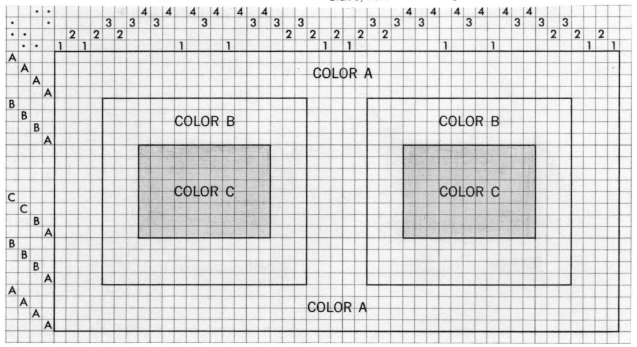

Center section (see gray tone) can be repeated as often as desired.

Bound-Weave Rugs

Like tapestry, bound weave is a flat, weft-faced structure, but unlike tapestry it is loom-controlled. Basically a twill, it has a pronounced right and wrong side. The patterns are formed by combinations of threading, treadling, and color. Because of the spacing of the warp and the threading arrangement, the colors beat down very closely over one another, emerging only in certain spots as part of the design. The weft must also be beaten down hard to make the structure firm; as a result, the rugs are very thick and a large amount of weft yarn is required.

Many patterns can be woven on the same threading draft. While the treadling sequence remains the same, the weft colors change according to the desired pattern. Experimentation with this weave is the only way to explore its many fascinating possibilities.

The rug sample shown in Figure 9-24 makes a good project to start from. It is woven with a warp of 8/3 Swedish linen set six threads per inch in a twelve-dent reed. The threads are spaced in every other dent, and two extra threads are added for each selvage. The weft is a blend of Swedish cow hair and wool.

The threading is:

1,2,1,2,3,2,3,4,3,4,1,4,3,4,1,4,3,4,3,2,3,2
repeat once, ending with 1,2,1

The treadling sequence is:

3-4—color for outline
1-4—color for inner edge
1-2—color for square
2-3—same color for square

The treadling sequence remains the same, but three

9-25. Rug in bound weave, soumak, and fringe by Jane Redman. This bound weave design is a traditional Scandinavian pattern known as "bound rosepath."

colors change according to the design: the color sequence repeats in the order shown in the draft to produce the block-within-a-block pattern. There are no long floats on either side, so the rug is reversible, though the design is different on the reverse.

This pattern is also illustrated in the wall hanging on page 166.

Other threadings can be used, including block, Summer and Winter, herringbone, broken twills, and point twills. Variations can also be made by combining bound weave with other techniques, as in the rug shown in Figure 9-25.

Stuffer Rugs

The stuffer rug has double-woven surfaces and is therefore completely reversible. An extra set of warp threads between the layers acts as stuffing and makes the weave extremely thick and durable. The stuffer warp does not show on the surface, but the weaving warp shows on the face and reverse of the rug.

The technique of making stuffer rugs was developed by Mary M. Atwater and published in *Handweaver and Craftsman*. Her directions, condensed by Lurene Stone, are presented here.

A horizontal loom with at least four harnesses (and preferably more) and two warp beams is needed. If a second warp beam is not available, the weaving warp may be wound into a chain and hung over the back of the loom, as shown in Figure 9-13.

The weaving warp should be strong wool or cotton of medium weight, and the color or colors should blend with the weft yarn. The stuffer warp should be carpet warp or other inexpensive cotton yarn. It may be of any color, since it does not show in the finished rug, but if it is coordinated with the weft yarns, then its ends can be included in the fringe when the rug is finished. The weft yarn should be heavy wool or cotton rug yarn in two contrasting colors. Each is wound on a separate shuttle. One or more strands may be used: three strands of Swedish cow hair and wool yarn make an excellent weft.

The weaving warp must be one and three-quarters times the length of the rug plus the usual allowance for tying and waste. The stuffer warp is as long as the rug, plus the allowance.

The setting for the weaving warp is five threads per inch in a ten- or fifteen-dent reed or six threads per inch in a twelve-dent reed. Two extra threads of weaving warp should be added on each side for selvages. The setting for the stuffer warp is twenty threads per inch in a ten- or fifteen-dent reed or twenty-four in a twelve-dent reed.

The stuffer warp is wound on one warp beam by sectional or chain warping. Wind the weaving warp on the other warp beam (or wind a number of small warp chains and hang them, properly weighted, at the back of the loom). Harnesses 1 and 2 are reserved for the

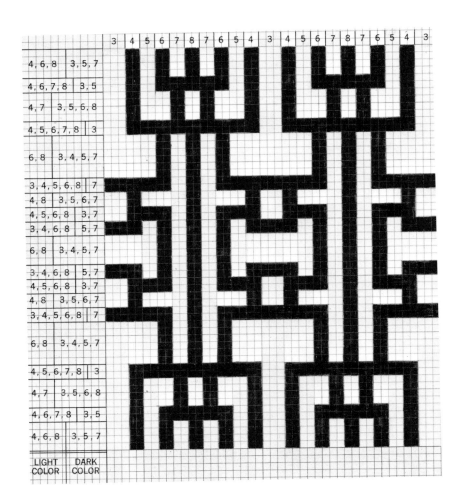

LIGHT COLOR	DARK COLOR
4,6,8	3,5,7
4,6,7,8	3,5
4,7	3,5,6,8
4,5,6,7,8	3
6,8	3,4,5,7
3,4,5,6,8	7
4,8	3,5,6,7
4,5,6,8	3,7
3,4,6,8	5,7
6,8	3,4,5,7
3,4,6,8	5,7
4,5,6,8	3,7
4,8	3,5,6,7
3,4,5,6,8	7
6,8	3,4,5,7
4,5,6,7,8	3
4,7	3,5,6,8
4,6,7,8	3,5
4,6,8	3,5,7

Top: 3 4 5 6 7 8 7 6 5 4 3 4 5 6 7 8 7 6 5 4 3

9-26. Stuffer rug by Diane Craig. Natural and dark gray handspun wool.

Left:
Draft for Fig. 9-26

Below:
A Profile draft showing arrangement and size of the blocks.

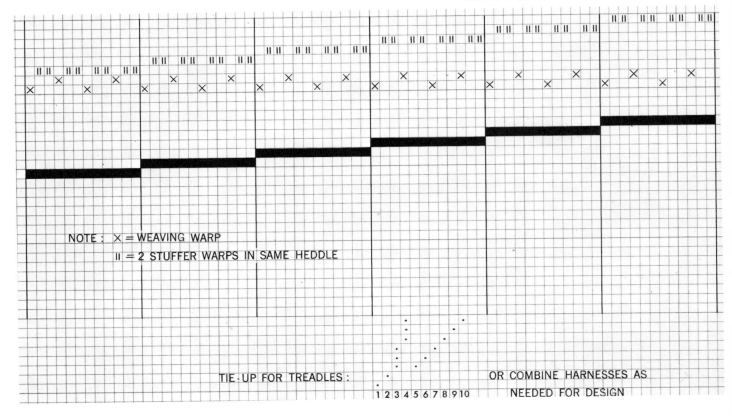

NOTE : X = WEAVING WARP

‖ = 2 STUFFER WARPS IN SAME HEDDLE

TIE-UP FOR TREADLES :

1 2 3 4 5 6 7 8 9 10

OR COMBINE HARNESSES AS

NEEDED FOR DESIGN

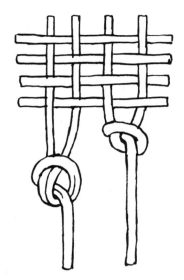

9-27. Overhand knot.

9-28. Double-hitch knot.

weaving warp and make the plain weave; therefore, the weaving warps are threaded alternately on the first two harnesses. The pattern is made by threading blocks on the remaining harnesses with the stuffer warp. Either warp may be threaded first, but be sure to leave heddles and dents for the other warp. Keep the tension on the weaving warp loose, on the stuffer warp tight.

The possible threading arrangements are similar to those used for Summer and Winter. The following example places block 1 on harness 3:

> harness 1—one weaving warp
> harness 3—two stuffer warps
> harness 3—two stuffer warps
> harness 2—one weaving warp
> harness 3—two stuffer warps
> harness 3—two stuffer warps

This threading is repeated for the desired width of the block. Note that there are always four stuffer warp threads between each weaving warp thread.

For a ten- or twelve-dent reed, the sleying would be:

> dent 1—one weaving warp
> dent 2—four stuffer warps
> dent 3—one weaving warp
> dent 4—four stuffer warps

and so on.

For a fifteen-dent reed, the sleying would be:

> dent 1—one weaving warp
> dent 2—two stuffer warps
> dent 3—two stuffer warps
> dent 4—one weaving warp

and so on.

Each row of design consists of four picks. For a solid color, the treadling sequence is:

> 1—weave color A
> 1 (plus all block harnesses)—weave color B
> 2—weave color A
> 2 (plus all block harnesses)—weave color B

For the pattern, the sequence is:

> 1 (plus desired block harnesses)—weave color A
> 1 (plus opposite block harnesses)—weave color B
> 2 (plus desired block harnesses)—weave color A
> 2 (plus opposite block harnesses)—weave color B

Repeat these four picks as often as needed to build up the block design. Change the block combination according to the design, and be sure to keep alternating the colors in the four picks.

FRINGES

If no fringe is desired, the woven edges of a rug may be turned under and sewn to the back of the rug. However, most rugs are finished with a fringe at each end. Several picks of tabby are woven at the beginning and end of the rug, and if a fringe is planned, approximately eight inches of warp yarn should be left in addition. After the rug is taken off the loom, the loose threads are tied together in pairs or small groups with an overhand knot (Figure 9-27).

If you wish to make the fringe from weft yarn instead of warp yarn, you can insert short lengths of weft yarn into the turned-under edge of the rug with double-hitch knots. A crochet hook is helpful for this method of making fringe (Figure 9-28).

161

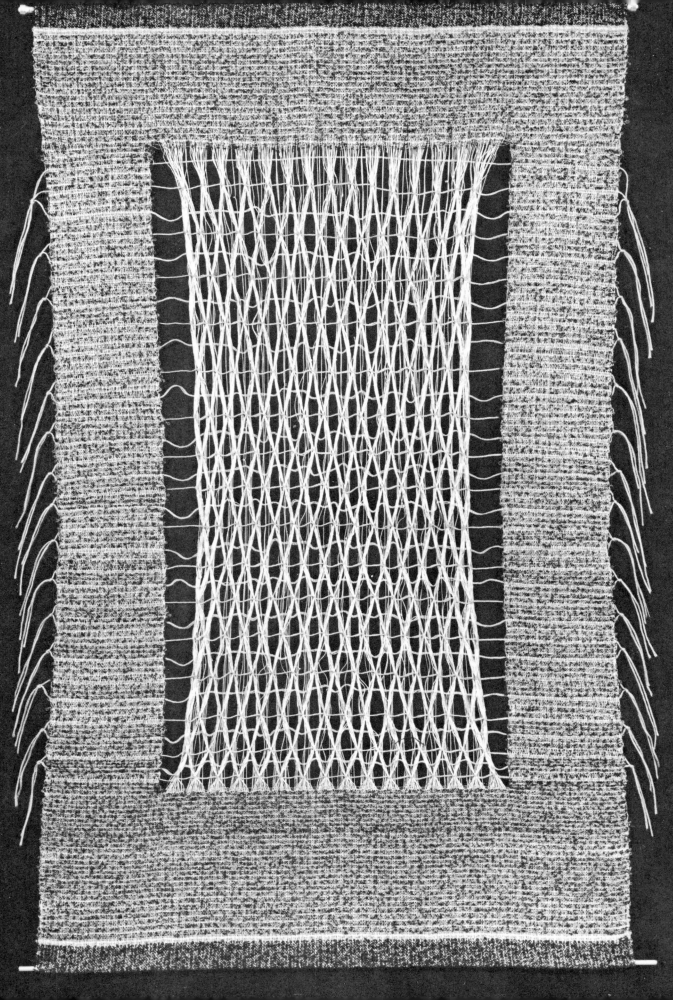

10

WALL HANGINGS

In none of its contemporary faces does weaving reflect more freedom, joy, and originality of design than in wall hangings, a category that is far more encompassing than its name implies. Today a wall hanging may be a piece of weaving that hangs on the wall, but it may also be one that is suspended from the ceiling or that stands by itself on the floor. This form of art is thus closely related to painting and sculpture but has in addition the flexibility and texture of the fibers, which, manipulated into forms and shapes by weaving, knitting, knotting, crocheting, or stitching, project the artist's ideas. The traditional yarns may be enriched and supplemented by unusual materials such as feathers, stones, shells, ceramics, or beads. Wall hangings may be shaped directly on the loom by techniques based on the weaver's previous experiences or taken off the loom to be elaborated with other free techniques; some are even fashioned entirely without the use of a loom.

The techniques used to make most of the hangings illustrated in this chapter can be identified by referring to preceding chapters. However, four techniques not previously described are used in some of the works shown and will be discussed here. They are laid-in weaving, tie-dye or painting, macramé or knotting, and finger weaving.

LAID-IN WEAVING

Laid-in weaving, or brocading, refers to a pattern thread that is "laid in" the same shed with a background thread. The pattern thread moves back and forth only within the area of its design, while the background threads run from selvage to selvage. Both yarns can be of the

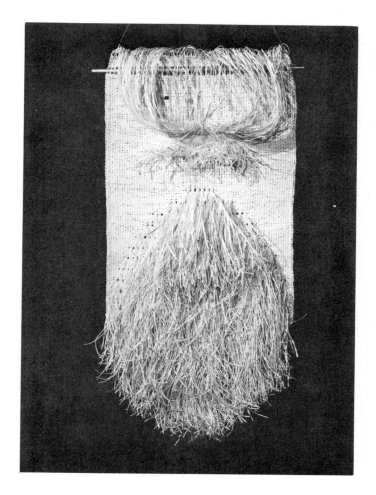

10-2. "White Peacock," hanging by Nell Znamierowski. Paper and plastic yarns. (Photo courtesy of The Art Institute of Chicago)

10-1. "Lace Weave," hanging by Else Regensteiner.
Yellow, brown, black, and gold linen and mohair.
(Photo: John W. Rosenthal)

10-5. "Tabs Hanging," hanging by Frank A. Muehlenbeck. Blue linen with can tabs. (Photo: Grand Rapids Art Museum)

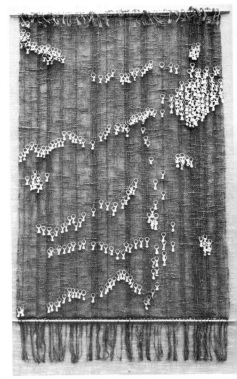

10-3. "Winged Pegasus," hanging by Lenore Tawney. (Photo courtesy of the artist and Fairweather Hardin Gallery)

10-4. "Sculptural Form," composition by Sharon Kouris. Natural and brown wool and tree trunk.

10-6. "Captured," hanging by Marcella Baumgaertner. Plain weave and rya loops with stained glass shells.

10-7. "The Bird," composition by Sharon Kouris.

10-8. "Mask," hanging
by Ted Hallman.

10-10. Hanging in HV technique by
Takeko Nomiya.

10-11. Hanging in HV technique by
Linda Howard.

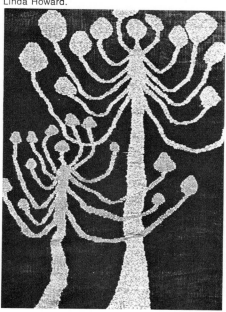

same weight and beaten tightly, making an opaque cloth, or the background threads can be much finer than the design threads and beaten lightly, which makes the background sheer with the design standing out clearly. The background thread has to be thrown across the warp first and the pattern thread laid on top of it. This is called the HV technique, from the Swedish *Halvgobelang* or half-tapestry. Figures 10-10 and 10-11 show patterns woven by this method. When intricate designs are desired, a pick-up stick is useful, but for simple patterns, flat shuttles on which the weft threads are wound are sufficient.

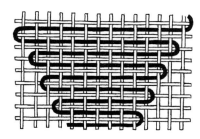

10-9. HV technique.

"Chichi," wall hanging in double weave with braided and tied threads on the top layer and plain weave on the bottom layer, by Else Regensteiner. (Photo: Roger Poznan, Brand Studio)

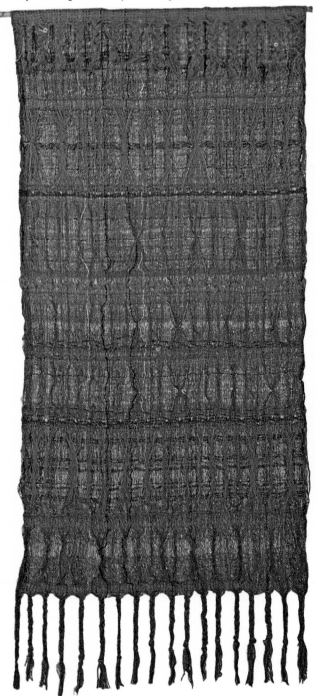

Wall hanging in bound weave by Astra Strobel. (Photo courtesy of the artist)

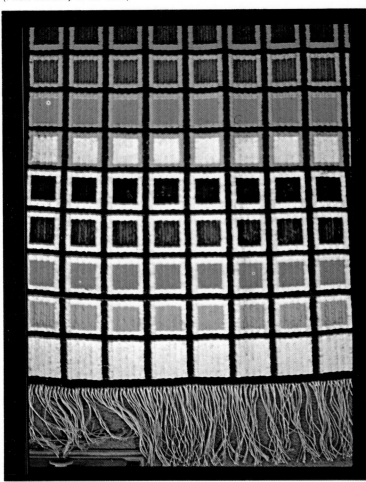

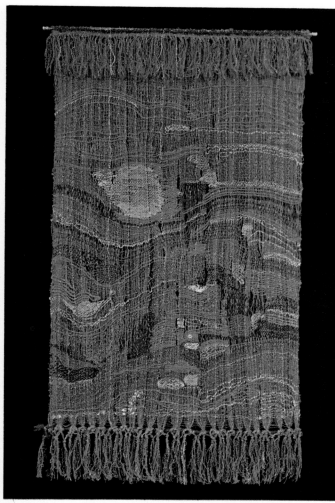

"Dazzling Journey," wall hanging in slit and interlocking tapestry techniques by Else Regensteiner. (Photo: John W. Rosenthal)

Wall hanging with buttons and shells by Else Regensteiner. The top layer is leno, the bottom layer is plain weave. (Photo: Roger Poznan, Brand Studio)

10-12. Tie-dyed warp chain from Santiago Atitlán, Guatemala, where weavers can buy skeins ready made in the market.

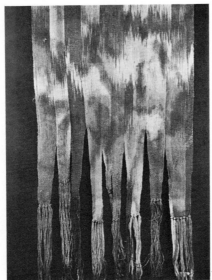

10-13. Hanging in random tie-dyed warp pattern by Linda Howard.

10-14. Silk fabric with elaborate *ikat* design from Cambodia. (Collection of Barbara Fine)

TIE-DYE AND PAINTING

Weavers frequently do not realize that exquisite effects can be achieved by applying paints and dyes directly to warp or weft threads. This technique is commonly seen in textiles from Indonesia, India, Africa, South and Central America, and Japan. Although known by a variety of names including *kasuri* (Japanese), *jaspé* and *chiné* (French), and *ikat* (Javanese), all tie-dye is basically the creation of mottled designs made by pre-dyed threads, usually silk or cotton. Tie-dye designs can be made in the warp or weft yarns.

For warp designs, the threads are measured in groups of eight or ten on a warping board and made into skeins that are stretched lengthwise on a frame or table. The part of the yarn that is to stay undyed is then wrapped tightly with yarns to prevent the dye from penetrating. When all the skeins are tied, they are taken off the frame or table and put into a dye bath. After thorough rinsing and drying, the wrappings are removed. If more colors are desired, the whole process is repeated, only this time the dyed parts are wrapped and the undyed places are colored. Typical tie-dyeing, however, involves only one dyeing. The warp is then put on the loom by chain warping. Frequently the tie-dyed groups of warp threads are alternated with plain colored bands of warp—this not only makes the fabric more colorful but also is easier, because fewer groups of threads have to be dyed.

Weft tie-dye is made the same way, the weft yarns being measured for the width of the warp. Patterns can be easily varied by arranging the spots of colors in different positions or by varying the width of the tie-dyed sections or the length of the wrapped and un-wrapped parts. Often warp and weft patterns are co-ordinated to make the spots and splashes meet or over-lap. These double patterns give elaborate and fasci-nating effects.

The kind of dye used for tie-dyeing depends on the fiber content of the yarn to be dyed. Most yarns can be colored with the aniline dyes sold in small packages in drug and grocery stores, and these are adequate for experimental work. However, they are usually not suffi-ciently lightfast for the serious craftsman, and acid dyes (for wool, silk, and nylon) and direct dyes (for cotton, rayon, and linen), available in weaving supply shops, are recommended for important projects.

10-15. Detail of warp-painted hanging by Richard Scrozynski.

Warp painting can be done with textile paints. Experiments on samples with colored inks and felt-tip pens have started many weavers on more ambitious projects. The color can be applied directly to the warp already stretched on the loom. In this case a piece of cardboard must be held under the warp threads in front of the beater while they are being painted. Only the short section between the beater and the front apron can be colored at one time, and the paint must dry before weaving can begin. Alternatively, the complete length of warp can be taped tightly to the surface of a table protected by paper and painted before it is put on the loom. It hardly need be said that the threads must be kept in meticulous order to transfer the design correctly.

KNOTTING

Figures 10-16 and 10-17 illustrate structures made without a loom. Some consist of long strands of yarn tied directly to a rod or branch with double-hitch knots that form an organic part of the hanging. The technique used in these works is generally known as macramé. It is an ancient art long known and used for a multitude of purposes in the Middle East, Europe, and Central and South America. Fishermen, sailors, and boy scouts are familiar with its basis and mainstay, the square knot. Contemporary handweavers have found that the technique of knotting is very congenial to their own technique of working directly with fibers. Many structures may be made with plain heavy jute, or linen or cotton cord.

10-16. "Dancer," hanging with macramé knotted in tubular form with loops by Leora K. Stewart. Beige jute and red wool.

10-17. "Rib Cage," hanging with wrapped and unravelled threads by Leora K. Stewart. Beige and natural jute with black and white wool.

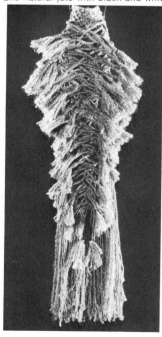

10-18. The steps in making a macramé knot.

10-19. Flat macramé knot.

10-20. Chain of macramé knots.

10-22. Hanging in macramé, weaving, and ceramic beads by Lois Lebov.

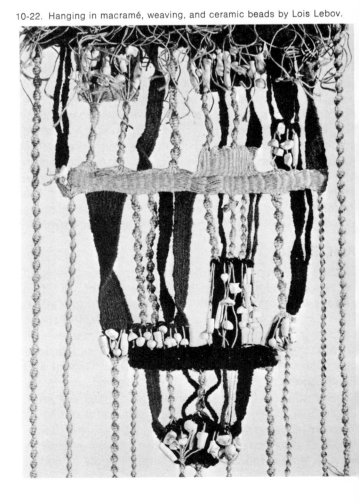

The macramé knot is made as illustrated in Figure 10-18. Four strands of yarn (or two doubled strands) are used for a single knot. Two strands form the center of the knot, and the two outside strands are tied around the center with a half-knot from the right side and a half-knot from the left side. When the knots are always started over or under from the same side, then the outside strands form a spiral around the core, resulting in a corkscrew twist. When the knots are started alternating from right and left, they form a flat square knot (Figure 10-19); when many knots are tied continuously, a rope results (Figure 10-20). If groups of four strands are knotted together in alternate knots, as illustrated in Figure 10-21, a lacy, netlike structure will result. (In her book *Macramé: The Art of Creative Knotting*, Virginia I. Harvey explains and describes many variations and uses of macramé that are of value for the weaver.)

10-21. Macramé knots in alternate arrangement.

FINGER WEAVING

The technique of finger weaving probably preceded that of loom weaving in the ancient world, and it was utilized in the construction of early shelters. In finger weaving, a desired number of threads are tied to a top rod with double-hitch knots or looped over a warp stick. Each thread serves for both warp and weft, as may be seen in Figure 10-24. Arrangements of colors form the patterns.

To weave a simple piece, tie eight threads to a stick, which can be left in the work afterwards as part of the hanging. (In Figure 10-24, the warp threads are brought down from a bunch and looped around a warp stick that can be removed after the weaving is completed.) The first warp thread on the left side becomes a weft and is taken over and under each warp until it arrives at the right side, where it again becomes a warp. The second thread starts the same way, moving from the left edge to the right, and the process is continued until the weaving is completed. In more complicated variations such as that shown in Figure 10-26, the weaving starts from the center and moves in opposite directions to either side.

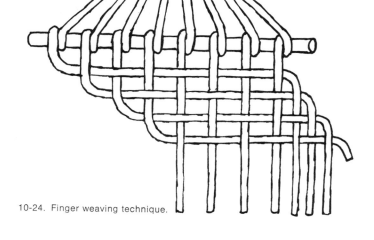

10-24. Finger weaving technique.

Below left:
10-25. Detail of finger-woven sash. (Photo courtesy of John Kennardh White)
Below right:
10-26. "Golden Flow," finger-woven hanging in seine twine by Carol Weston.

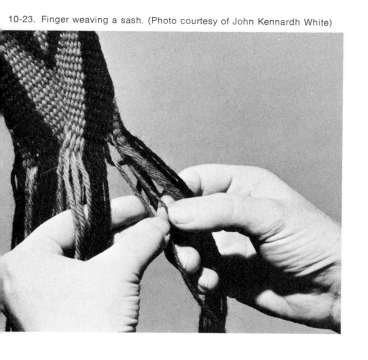

10-23. Finger weaving a sash. (Photo courtesy of John Kennardh White)

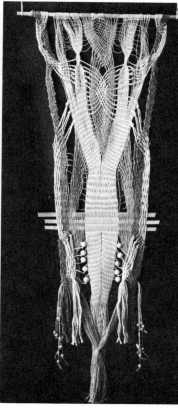

10-27. "Jewel in the Grass," hanging by Nell Znamierowski. Paper and metal. (Collection of The Art Institute of Chicago. Photo: Ferdinand Boesch)

10-28. "Venus Night Flight," hanging by Loraine Gonzalez. Nylon yarns and lucite rods. (Photo courtesy of the artist)

Many of the techniques described in this chapter can be used and combined in very imaginative ways. In the creation of wall hangings a certain degree of playfulness is appropriate, and should be encouraged. It is the same creative play that helps children to grow, to experience, and to express themselves. No play or experiment can culminate in a work of art every time, of course. Even the loftiest idea is worthless when its execution is poor. Vision and craftsmanship must go hand in hand to create beautiful pieces with integrity.

The illustrations in this book have been selected as representative examples of the artist-craftsman's work. Some are simple, some are complicated; all show genuine understanding of the weaver's great potential strength and demonstrate that the oldest craft can be the newest art.

10-29. "Feather Tapestry," hanging by Jane Redman. Red and orange wool with feathers and shells.

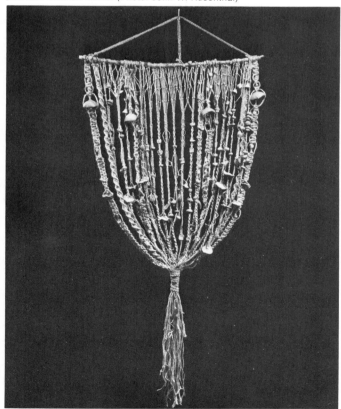

10-31. "Guinea," hanging by Terry Illes. Red wool and natural guinea-hen feathers. (Photo courtesy of Marna Johnson)

10-30. "How does your garden grow?" hanging by Libby Crawford. (Photo: Associated Artists Advertising Agency)

10-32. "Siam II," macramé hanging by Else Regensteiner. Linen and jute with ceramic forms. (Photo: John W. Rosenthal)

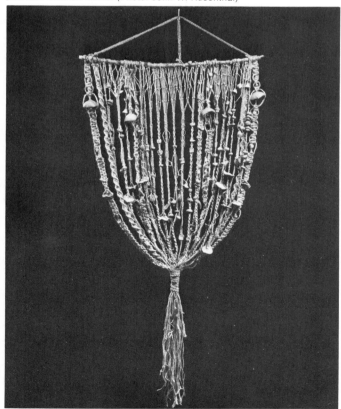

APPENDIX I

THE BACK-STRAP LOOM

Text and Photographs
by Madeleine Smith

MAKING THE LOOM: MATERIALS AND PROCEDURE

Warp Beam and Breast Beam (Figure A-1, *b* and *i*)

Two pieces of dowel, ¾″ in diameter and 16″ long or about 4″ longer than the width of the piece to be woven. Make a ¼″-wide groove and taper the dowels to a diameter of about ½″ about 1″ in from each end.

Holder for Rolled Web on Breast Beam (Figure A-2)

One piece of dowel, ¾″ or ½″ in diameter and the same length as warp and breast beams. Taper the dowel as for warp and breast beams. This piece is used to hold the web in place against the breast beam when it is rolled forward. It is not used with a very short warp.

Shed Sticks

Two pieces of wood about ⅛″ thick and ¾″ wide, the same length as warp and breast beams. Drill holes in the ends so that the sticks can be tied together after being placed in the cross.

Heddle Stick (Figure A-1g)

One piece of dowel, ⅜″ in diameter, the same length as warp and breast beams. Make a ⅛″-wide shallow groove ¼″ in from each end of the stick.

Countershed Stick (Figure A-1e)

One flat piece of wood about ¼″ thick and 1¼″-2″ wide, the same length as warp and breast beams. Drill a hole about ⅛″ in diameter at each end. A cardboard tube, 2″-3″ in diameter may be used instead.

Sword or Batten (Figure A-1f)

One piece of hard wood about ¼″ thick and 2″ wide, about 4″ longer than the width of the loom. A wooden venetian blind slat or similar piece of wood may be used instead. Taper to form a thin, knifelike edge along one side.

Back Strap (Figure A-1k)

A 6″ strip of 36″-wide cotton, knotted at both ends, or 3½″ furniture webbing, 30″ long. Fold to 1¾″ at the ends and sew both ends firmly about ½″ from the edge. Open out to full width and turn seam to wrong side; the ends are now pointed. For each end, double a stout cord about 30″ long and run the ends of it into the point on

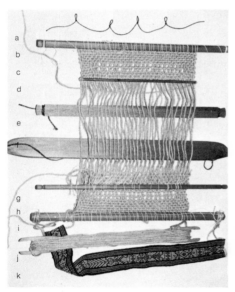

A-1. Loom set up to weave a place mat. Wood parts by Harold Power, East Chicago, Indiana.

a. Knotted heddle cord.
b. Warp beam.
c. First weaving.
d. Template (shown here on right side).
e. Countershed stick.
f. Sword.
g. Heddle stick.
h. Second weaving.
i. Breast beam.
j. Shuttle.
k. Back strap (made from a straight band).

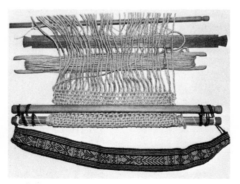

A-2. Holder for rolled web.
A-3. First cord in position to hold warp loops to beam.

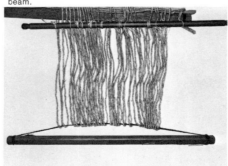

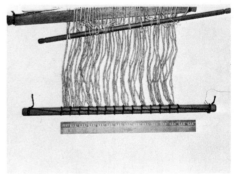

A-4. Second cord buttonholed in place on beam.
A-5. Third cord wound around beam to spread the warp evenly.

the right side to the underside. Leave a loop of about 12″ extending out from the point. Knot the cord ends under the point on the wrong side so the loop will not pull out under tension.

Stretcher or Template (Figure A-1d)

A piece of bamboo or hollow garden stake about ¼″ in diameter, the same length, exactly, as the width of the weaving. A ¾″ finishing nail at each end of the stretcher is caught in a loop of selvage to keep the full weaving width of the piece. The stretcher is attached to the underside of the web after a few rows have been woven and is moved up every few rows.

Finishing the Loom

The wood pieces of the back-strap loom will look attractive if they are rubbed down with a little turpentine and burnt umber. The sword should be polished.

Shuttles

Flat shuttles of various widths, longer than weaving width.

Cords

A sturdy four-ply jute cord (like that used for tying parcels) may be used for attaching the back strap to the breast beam and tying the warp beam to an anchor. Number 6 seine twine is suggested for making heddles and #9 for all other cords. In addition to the heddle cord, you will need a total of ten cords: two pieces about 12″ longer than the warp and breast beams for tying the loop end of the warp to the beams (Figure A-3); two pieces for buttonhole stitching the warp to the beams (Figure A-4)—if you are using ¾″ dowels, allow 4″ of cord for each inch of weaving width, plus a yard or more extra; two pieces 3½ yards long (longer for a wide warp) to wind around the dowels to spread the warp evenly (Figure A-5); two pieces about 30″ long to tie the back strap to the breast beam; and two pieces about 36″ long for tying the warp beam to the anchor (Figure A-6). To make the inverted Y for tying the warp beam to the anchor, double one piece of cord and knot the ends together. Knot a loop at the end of the other cord and slip the first cord, doubled, through this loop.

To estimate how much cord you need for tying the heddles, multiply half the number of warp ends plus one by 6″ and add a yard or so for good measure. Or tie the required number of heddle knots directly from a ball of cord.

Tying the Heddle

To tie a heddle *using knots,* as illustrated in Figure A-1a, you will need a measuring gauge made from a piece of 1″ x 6″ cardboard or a ruler. Measure a 6″ length of #6 seine twine, carpet warp, or another hard cord. Turn the length coming from the ball back onto another 6″ length and make an overhand loop knot (Figure A-7) about ⅝″ from the end of the loop. (If a large dowel is used for a heddle stick, the loop must be made large enough to slide easily

on the stick.) From the end of this loop measure another 6″, turn the cord back as before, and make a second loop about ⅝″ from the loop end. Continue until you have tied one more loop than half the number of warp ends (there must be one loop outside the right and left warp ends to hold the heddle stick in place).

The same cord may be used over again: if it is too long for another project, cut it to the right length halfway between knots and reserve the extra length for future use.

To tie a heddle *without knots,* pass the heddle cord through the first shed, bringing one end to the left side of the warp. (Note: the second shed is made by the shed sticks.) Place the right end of the heddle stick at the left side of the warp and tie the end of the cord loosely around the near end of the stick. Starting from the left-hand side, pick up the heddle cord in the shed from between the first and second warp ends, which rest on top of the shed stick. Twist the cord once and pass the loop onto the heddle stick. Pick up the heddle cord from the shed between the second and third warp ends on top of the shed stick, twist, and place on heddle stick. Continue in this manner, ending with the heddle cord tied to the stick at the right-hand side of the last warp end. If the cord is tied too tightly on the ends of the stick, the heddles on the outer edges shorten as the stick is rolled, making a very narrow shed. The heddle cord must then be loosened and straightened out.

INSTRUCTIONS FOR WEAVING A PLACE MAT WITH FOUR SELVAGES

Coarse yarns are suggested for first projects on the back-strap loom. Jute, sisal, 8/8 cotton (Curl Bros., Toronto), Kentucky All Purpose Yarn (Item 301), and many others are suitable; carpet warp woven with a heavy weft will make firm material if well beaten down. In the project described here, a heavy brown jute was used for warp and weft. Any fiber should be checked for shrinkage: the sample shown was made with a warp 13½″ wide and 20″ long and measured 12¼″ x 18″ after washing.

For the place mat, 82 warp ends are used, set 6 ends per inch; 42 heddle knots are needed. The procedure is as follows:

(1) Draw a line around the circumference of a 16″ dowel at its center (that is, 8″ in from the ends). Then make two more marks around the circumference of the dowel 6¾″ to the right and left of the center line. Place a second dowel against the first and make identical marks on it. These are the breast and warp beams.

(2) Make a warp 20″ long with a single cross. Tie cross and both ends of the warp before removing it from the warping board Tie shed sticks at the cross, removing the first ties. Tie the shed sticks together through the holes at the ends.

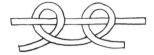

A-8. Clove hitch.

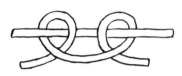

A-9. Single ring hitch.

A-10.

(3) Pass a 28″ cord through the loops at one end of the warp (see Figure A-3) and attach it with a clove hitch (Figure A-8) to each end of the stick, tightening the cord. Repeat with another cord at the other end of the warp, removing the ties. At the end of the warp that has two single strands (the first and last threads of the warp), tie the loose ends to the cord holding the warp loops against the beam. (When the weaving is finished, the ends are untied and darned into the web.)

(4) The next steps are easier to carry out with the warp under tension. Attach the loop ends of the inverted Y cord to the warp beam with a single ring hitch (Figure A-9). Tie the single end of the Y to a post, door handle, or a C clamp attached to a table. Attach the end loops of the back strap to the breast beam with another single ring hitch. Place the back strap low on your hips.

(5) Tie one end of a 3-yard-long cord to the left end of the breast beam (under the back-strap cord) with a clove hitch. (Other knots can be used, but this is the easiest to untie.)

(6) Starting at the left, with the cord make a buttonhole stitch (Figure A-10) around the dowel at the mark to the left of the warp, being sure to catch in the cord holding the loop ends of warp (see Figure A-4). Count off six ends (three loops); place a second buttonhole stitch exactly 1″ from the first. (The stick may be marked off in inches, but a ruler works well as a gauge.) Tighten the cord at the inch mark and continue, until the required number of ends per inch are placed between each stitch. There will be four ends at the right-hand edge, and the distance between the last two stitches will be ⅔″ instead of 1″.

(7) Now tie one end of another 3-yard-long cord at the left-hand side of the breast beam, again using a clove hitch placed under the back-

A-6. Inverted Y cord.

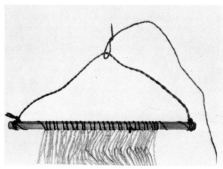

A-7. Overhand loop knot.

A-11. Loom with jute mat partially woven. Note heddle stick and weaving at both ends.

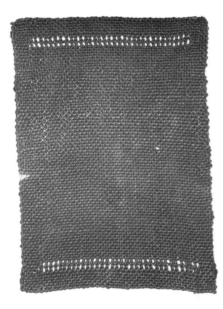

A-12. Finished mat. Note the four selvages.

strap tie so that the back strap can be removed from the beam easily. Wind this cord around the dowel several times; then pass it through each single warp loop. On this warp, there are three loops in each inch. Continue winding the cord in the same way for the full width of the warp, ending with a few turns around the dowel before tying the cord on the right-hand side of the breast beam (again under the back-strap tie). Space the warp ends as evenly as possible as you wind the cord, and keep the cord tight.

(8) Remove back-strap and warp-beam cords. Turn the loom upside down and refasten the cords. Buttonhole the second end with the third cord; then wind the fourth cord on to spread the warp, as described in step 7.

(9) To attach the heddle stick, pass the knotted heddle cord through the first shed, bringing the first loop out to the left of the first warp end. Place the right end of the heddle stick at the left side of the warp, slipping the first loop on it. Pick up the second heddle loop between the first and second warp ends and slip it on the stick. The first warp end will be caught between the first and second loops on the heddle stick. Continue picking up the heddle cord loops and placing them on the heddle stick, one loop for every warp end on top of the shed stick, until you reach the right side of the warp. The last loop must be picked up on the outside of the last warp end. Tie a cord along the length of the heddle stick to keep the loops from slipping.

(10) Place the countershed stick in place. Remove the shed sticks holding the cross. Tie a cord along the countershed stick so that it cannot slip out of the warp. Tie it loosely enough so that the stick can be turned on its edge.

(11) Wind a shuttle with enough weft to weave about twenty-four rows, or 4″.

For weaving, the breast beam should rest against or near the body, and the back strap should be low down on your hips. A half-hitch of the cord onto the beam will bring the breast beam closer, if necessary. It is a matter of preference whether the warp beam is tied higher than the breast beam, or if the warp is horizontal. In order to avoid fatigue, sit with good posture. Tension the warp by leaning back slightly. When weaving on the heddle stick shed, lessen the tension by leaning forward slightly.

(12) Place the first shot of weft in the shed. Tuck in the weft end. Change the shed and beat weft in well with the sword. Pass shuttle through shed and change shed. Beat well. After weaving several rows in this manner, attach the template as directed, and move it forward every few rows.

(13) After six or seven rows have been woven, ending on the right-hand side, weave one row of leno.

(14) Continue weaving in plain weave until the piece measures about 4″, beating the weft in as well as possible. Then break off the weft.

(15) Wind a shuttle with enough weft to finish the mat. In order to weave the four selvages, turn the loom upside down and move the countershed stick to the back of the heddle stick. Use a second stick to keep its shed open until the countershed stick has been untied, moved, and retied. Weave as before, including leno row. Continue until the shed becomes too narrow for the shuttle and sticks; replace them with narrower shuttles and sticks until it is no longer possible to pass a shuttle or stick through the shed. The last rows are darned in with a large-eyed needle. Keep the same number of rows per inch, and end with a row in the opposite shed to the last used in the first half of the weaving. Tuck in the weft ends on opposite sides of the mat, if possible, to avoid having two ends on the same side. Remove the mat from the loom. The cords may be saved for another warp, or cut off.

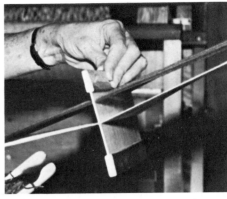

A-13. Rigid heddle is depressed to open shed.

WEAVING WITH A RIGID HEDDLE

Sometimes a rigid heddle (or heddle **reed**) may be used instead of a heddle stick. The rigid heddle is a comb made of metal or wood. It consists of slats, each with a hole in the center. The warp is threaded alternately one thread through a hole, the next through the slit between adjacent slats. By moving the heddle up, one shed is produced; by pressing it down, the alternate shed is made. If the rigid heddle is strong, it can also be used as a beater.

The warp is made in the usual manner and chained. Place shed sticks in place at the cross, and tie them. Cut the loops at the end near the shed sticks and thread them through the rigid heddle; then remove the shed sticks. Attach the back strap to the breast beam and around your hips. The cut ends of warp are attached to the beam as on an ordinary loom.

The rigid heddle is easy to use with a long warp—for instance, to weave projects such as belts and scarves.

WEAVING WITH A LONG WARP

A very long warp can not be stretched for its full length between the breast and warp beams. Therefore, other arrangements have to be made. The warp is made in the way described previously and attached to the breast beam in the usual way. The end that would be attached to the warp beam, however, is treated the following way:

Make an overhand loop knot on the whole warp a yard away from the breast beam. Fasten this with a stout cord to a stationary object that will hold it under tension. Finish the warp arrangements with heddle sticks and countershed stick as usual, while the loom is attached to you by the back strap.

Start weaving with some strips of cardboard or a heavy yarn in order to spread the warp to its correct width. Then proceed with weaving as long as the shed can be reached conveniently. When the time comes to roll the web on to the breast beam, use a second stick the length of the breast beam to hold the web tightly to it (see Figure A-2). This stick must be secured tightly by winding some cord in figure-eight fashion over and under breast beam and stick at both ends. As the weaving proceeds, this stick will have to be untied and tied to the breast beam again. Release the other end of the warp gradually as needed to retain sufficient weaving space and a good tension.

APPENDIX II

FIGURING YARDAGE FOR WARP AND WEFT

HOW TO FIGURE WARP YARDAGE FOR A PLAIN WARP BEAM

(1) Determine length and width of material to be woven and number of warp ends per inch. Remember that an extra yard of warp that cannot be woven must be added for waste.

(2) Multiply width (in inches) by number of ends per inch to obtain the total number of threads in the warp.

(3) If the entire warp is to be the same color, multiply the number of ends by the length of the warp for the total yardage of warp yarn needed.

(4) If a color sequence is planned, divide the number of threads in the sequence into the total number of warp threads to obtain the number of sequences to be repeated across the warp.

(5) Next, count the number of threads of each color in one sequence and multiply by the number of sequences. This will give you the number of times each color appears across the warp—that is, the number of warp ends of each color.

(6) Multiply each color total by the length of the warp to obtain the total yardage needed for each color.

(7) For selvages, two (or more) additional threads are used for the outside edges of the warp. Multiply the number of selvage threads by the total length of the warp to obtain the yardage needed.

(8) If the color sequence is a simple repeat of two, three, or four threads, you can work out the total yardage for the entire warp as in step 3 and divide by a half, a third, a quarter, etc. to obtain the yardage for each color.

To give an example—for a piece that is to be twenty inches wide and five yards long, with a five-thread repeat of one black thread, two white threads, and two gray threads, set fifteen threads to the inch, with two selvage threads for each side of the warp, the yardage is calculated as follows:

20 inches x 15 ends per inch = 300 threads across the warp
  300 ÷ 5 = 60 color repeats
  1 black thread × 60 = 60 black threads
  2 white threads × 60 = 120 white threads
  2 gray threads × 60 = 120 gray threads
  60 × 5 yards = 300 yards black thread
  120 × 5 yards = 600 yards white thread
  120 × 5 yards = 600 yards gray thread
  4 selvage threads × 5 yards = 20 yards selvage thread

HOW TO FIGURE WARP YARDAGE FOR A SECTIONAL WARP BEAM (TWO-INCH SECTIONS)

(1) Determine length and width of material to be woven and number of warp ends per inch. Use a reed to fit, or adjust the number of threads to the dents in the reed.

(2) Multiply the number of ends per inch by two to determine the number of threads in a two-inch section. Try to fit the color sequence repeat evenly into the number of threads needed for a two-inch section.

(3) Divide the number of threads in the color sequence into the number of threads in the two-inch section to determine the number of repeats in each section.

(4) Divide the width of the warp by two to determine the number of two-inch sections across the warp.

(5) One spool is needed for each thread in a two-inch section. To determine the yardage to be wound on each spool, multiply the number of sections by the length of the warp and add several extra yards.

(6) Divide the spools into color groups by multiplying the number of repeats in a two-inch section by the number of threads of each color.

(7) Wind each spool with necessary yardage.

(8) For two selvage threads added to each side of the warp, wind two spools with thread twice the length of the warp plus a few extra yards for waste. (The selvage threads are added on the outside of the warp; they are *not* calculated with the repeats.) These spools are added first to the one, then to the other outside section of the warp before these sections are rolled on to the beam.

To give an example—for a piece that is to be thirty-six inches wide and five yards long, with a color sequence of eight threads (three blue, two black, three red), set twenty threads to the inch (two threads per dent in a ten-dent reed), the yardage is calculated as follows:

20 ends per inch × 2 = 40 threads per 2-inch section
36 inches (width of warp) ÷ 2 = 18 2-inch sections across the warp (each spool is used 18 times)
18 × 5 yards (length of warp) = 90 yards + 5 yards extra = 95 yards per spool
40 ÷ 8 threads per color sequence = 5 repeats per section
5 repeats × 3 blue threads = 15 blue spools
5 repeats × 2 black threads = 10 black spools
5 repeats × 3 red threads = 15 red spools
15 × 95 yards = 1,425 yards of blue thread
10 × 95 yards = 950 yards of black thread
15 × 95 yards = 1,425 yards of red thread
4 selvage threads × 5 yards = 20 yards selvage thread (on two *extra* spools)

HOW TO FIGURE WEFT YARDAGE

(1) Make a sample of the pattern.

(2) If the weft is to be of one color and one yarn only, count the number of picks per inch and multiply this by the width of the material. The result is the number of inches of weft used in one inch of warp—which is the same as the yardage of weft used in one yard of warp. Multiply this by the number of yards to be woven to obtain the total yardage of yarn needed for

(3) If various colors or yarns are to be used in the weft, examine one inch of weft and count the number of times each color or thread repeats. Multiply each total by the width of the material. The result is the number of inches of each color or yarn used in one inch or yard of the pattern. Then multiply each by the number of yards to be woven.

To give an example—for a piece of woven fabric that is to be forty inches wide and six yards long, with one color weft that beats down to twenty picks per inch, the yardage is calculated as follows:
  20 × 40 = 800 inches of weft per inch of warp or yards per yard
  800 × 6 yards = 4,800 yards needed for the weft

For a piece with the same measurements but with a yarn sequence of eight blue cotton threads plus three yellow wool threads plus four gold metallic threads plus five black bouclé threads (a total of twenty threads per inch of weft), the yardage is calculated as follows:
  8 blue threads × 40 = 320 inches of weft per inch of warp or yards per yard
  3 yellow threads × 40 = 120 inches per inch or yards per yard
  4 gold threads × 40 = 160 inches per inch or yards per yard
  5 black threads × 40 = 200 inches per inch or yards per yard
  320 × 6 yards = 1,920 yards blue thread needed for the weft
  120 × 6 yards = 720 yards yellow thread
  160 × 6 yards = 960 yards gold thread
  200 × 6 yards = 1,200 yards black thread

APPENDIX III

CONVERTING TIE-UPS FOR SINKING SHED LOOMS

To convert the tie-up for a rising shed (jack-type loom) for use with a sinking shed (counter-balanced loom), reverse the tie-up. Make a new draft in which the blank spaces of the rising shed draft are filled in and the filled-in spaces are left empty, as illustrated in the accompanying drafts. In the sinking shed loom, a harness simply stays up instead of being raised, because the opposite harnesses are pulled down. The weave remains exactly the same.

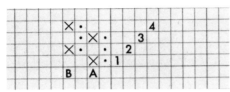

rising shed

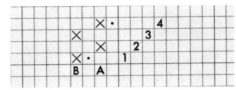

sinking shed

APPENDIX IV

VARIATIONS IN SYSTEMS AND SYMBOLS OF DRAFTING

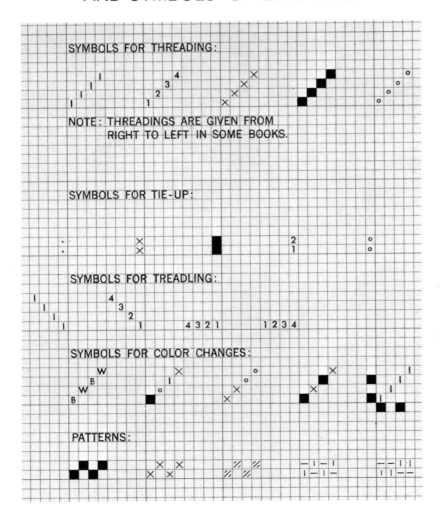

SYMBOLS FOR THREADING:

NOTE: THREADINGS ARE GIVEN FROM RIGHT TO LEFT IN SOME BOOKS.

SYMBOLS FOR TIE-UP:

SYMBOLS FOR TREADLING:

SYMBOLS FOR COLOR CHANGES:

PATTERNS:

APPENDIX V

PRACTICAL NOTES

HOW TO KEEP REPEATS EVEN

When you are weaving a material with a plaid or other pronounced color repeat, keep a card or tape measure with the repeat size marked on it and check the pattern from time to time so that the repeats remain even and do not grow larger or smaller with different beating. Tension should be released slightly when weaving stops for the day.

MEASURING YARDAGE DURING WEAVING

As you weave, mark the weft yardage along the edge of the material. Mark half yards with blue thread, full yards with red. (It is a good practice to count nineteen inches per half yard to allow for shrinkage.) By marking the yardage in this way, you can avoid having to unroll the material to check the amount you have woven.

WARP DRESSING

If a fuzzy wool gets sticky on the loom, be patient and clear the shed between reed and heddles by hand rather than by moving the beater back and forth. If the threads really need to be strengthened, apply a warp dressing. Boil linseeds in water until it reaches a consistency of thin starch, strain the liquid, and brush on the warp.

This dressing can also be used for linen warps, and chain warps may be dipped in it (and dried) before they are put on the loom.

HOW TO MEND BROKEN AND KNOTTED WARP THREADS

To mend a broken warp thread, pull the front end of the broken thread out of the dent toward the woven web and the other end out of the heddle toward the back of the loom. Measure a new length of warp thread so that it is long enough to reach from the front to the back beam and add to this about ten inches. Thread this repair thread from the front of the loom, through the heddle and dent left empty, to the back of the loom. Put a straight pin into the web about an inch below your last pick so that it lies parallel to the weft. Wind the repair thread around it in figure-eight fashion. Tie the other (long) end in the back to the old warp thread in a loop knot so that it has the same tension as the rest of the warp, and leave it hanging.

As the weaving proceeds, the loop knot will move toward the harnesses. When it reaches them, open it. Now the original thread can replace the repair thread in the heddle and dent. Pull the repair thread toward the front and

GLOSSARY

FOR THE WEAVER

leave it there; it can be darned in later. Wind the original thread around another straight pin to secure it in the right place and tension, and proceed with the weaving.

When weaving is finished, before the cloth is taken off the loom, remove the pins and weave the ends of the threads into the web with a large needle.

If a warp thread becomes knotted, cut the knot out and proceed as though the thread had been broken.

HOW TO CORRECT A THREADING MISTAKE

Sometimes, when testing the shed after threading and sleying are completed, the weaver finds that the shed is obstructed by warp threads that make the passage of the shuttle impossible. This is usually caused by a crossing of two warp threads between the heddle and the reed. To correct it, untie the small bunch of threads from the apron stick in front of the loom and slowly pull both crossed threads out of the reed towards the back. When they are crossed between their two heddles, pull them out of the heddles and rethread them in their proper place in heddles and dents. Retie on apron stick in the right tension.

Less frequently, but more subtle to detect, are warp threads threaded through the heddles in the wrong order, which causes a mistake in the fabric if uncorrected. Often you can insert a repair heddle in the place on the harness where the offending thread was supposed to be. Pull the thread out of the reed and heddle from the back and rethread it in the repair heddle on the correct harness.

To make a repair heddle, measure a piece of cotton warp so that it is twice the length of a heddle and add about 5 extra inches. Fold this thread over the top bar on the harness in exactly the place where it is needed. Even it out so that it is doubled in the middle. Tie it loosely (so that it can slide) with a square knot to the top bar of the harness. Make an overhand knot from both pieces for the top of the heddle eye, carefully judging the right height by the other heddles. The eye of the repair heddle must be exactly even with the eyes of the other heddles on the harnesses. Leave space for the eye, and make another overhand knot for the bottom of the eye. Tie the heddle with a square knot to the bottom bar of the harness. Trim the ends if necessary. Thread the warp thread through the eye in the usual manner. Rethread in the empty space left in the reed and retie on apron stick in the right tension.

Commercial repair heddles, made of steel, can be used. These heddles have open ends and snap on to the top and bottom bar of the harness.

GLOSSARY OF LOOMS

Back-Strap Loom—Warp is stretched between two rods, one attached to a stationary object, the other to the waist of the weaver. String heddles and shed sticks are used. (See Chapter 1.)

Back-Strap Loom with Rigid Heddle—Shed is made by a rigid comb or reed made of wood or metal and consisting of slats, each with a hole in the center. Warp is threaded alternating one thread through a hole, the next through the slit (or slot) between adjacent slats. By moving the rigid heddle up, one shed is produced; by moving it down, the opposite shed is produced. (See appendix, "The Back-Strap Loom".)

Card-Loom—A series of square cardboard cards with four holes that act as heddles. Used for narrow warps. The weaves are warp-faced. Work done on a card loom is sometimes called tablet or card weaving.

Counterbalanced Loom—Harnesses are lowered when treadle is pressed. (See Chapter 1.)

Dobby Loom—A drawloom on which small figures can be woven mechanically. Individual or groups of warp threads are pulled up by the dobby arrangement, a machine on top of the loom. Originally a "dobby boy" or "draw boy" sitting on top of the loom pulled up the warp threads. Now the dobby loom is usually an industrial power loom.

Double-Tie-Up or Countermarch Loom—Combines action of both jack-type and counterbalanced looms. Has two sets of lams, one upper, one lower; as one set pulls the harnesses down, the other set raises the rest of the harnesses. (See Chapter 1.)

Double Warp-Beam Loom—Has two warp beams, one below the other, used to adjust the tension of two sets of warp threads.

Draw Loom—Horizontal loom with an extra set of pattern harnesses behind the regular set. The pattern harnesses are controlled by separate sets of hand levers or pulleys.

Fly-Shuttle Loom—Loom with an arrangement on both sides of the beater by which the shuttle can be pushed back and forth between two boxes by hand or power mechanism.

Folding Loom—Loom that can be folded for moving or storage.

Foot Loom or Foot-Power Loom—Loom operated by foot treadles. (See Chapter 1.)

Frame Loom—Square, rectangular, or circular frame with wooden or metal nails across which threads are strung. Weft is worked in with a needle or the fingers.

Horizontal Loom—Any loom on which the warp runs horizontally from front to back.

Inkle Loom—Small wooden loom for narrow band weaving. Consists of a frame, pegs, and one set of string heddles. Warp threads are wound and threaded at the same time. The weaves are warp-faced.

Jack-Type Loom—Harnesses are raised when treadle is pressed. (See Chapter 1.)

Jacquard Loom—Mechanical power loom on which intricate patterns are made with the help of perforated cards. The cards are punched according to the design. Needles and hooks falling through the holes mechanically regulate, in connection with cords, rods, and other devices, the raising of warp-thread combinations.

Navajo Indian Loom—Upright loom with adjustable frame, one set of string heddles, shed sticks, and rollers for winding the woven cloth on the bottom beam.

Power Loom—Commercial loom driven by electricity or other power. Shuttles are thrown through the shed automatically, and raising and lowering of the harnesses, beating, and rolling of warp and cloth beams are mechanically controlled.

Rigid Loom—Loom that cannot be folded.

Rug Loom—Upright loom with two sheds often made with string heddles and shed sticks and bars on top and bottom on which warp is wound. Used for making knotted pile and flat rugs. Also, a heavy horizontal loom.

Table Loom—Harnesses operated by finger treadles. (See Chapter 1.)

Tapestry Loom—(1) Gobelin Loom: vertical loom with two sheds and string heddles, worked with small bobbins or butterflies and comb. (2) Aubusson Loom: horizontal loom with two harnesses and two foot treadles, worked with small bobbins and comb. (3) Contemporary vertical two-harness loom, with two foot treadles, and beater with reed. Worked with small bobbins, butterflies, or flat shuttles.

Upright Loom—Any loom on which the warp runs vertically from top to bottom.

Vertical Loom—Same as an upright loom.

GLOSSARY OF WEAVING TERMS

Apron—Fabric or sticks attached to warp and cloth beams.

Back Beam—Back rail on loom.

Basse Lisse—See Low Warp.

Beater (Batten)—Swinging beam that holds the reed and beats the weft threads into the warp.

Boat shuttle—Shuttle with hollowed-out part to hold small spool with weft thread.

Bobbin—Small spool inserted in shuttle on which weft threads are wound.

Bobbin Winder—Device for winding spools or bobbins by hand or electricity.

Breast Beam—Front rail on loom.

Cloth Beam—Front roller on loom on which woven fabric is wound.

Color pattern—pattern formed by combination of weaves and colors.

Comb—Forked wooden or metal piece used to beat weft threads into warp. See also Beater, Sword.

GLOSSARY OF WEAVING TERMS (Continued)

Corduroy—Pile weave with ridges. Pile can be cut or looped.

Cross—Criss-crossing of warp threads to keep them in order during warping. Also called lease.

Cross Rods—See Lease Rods.

Dents—Open spaces in the reed through which warp threads pass.

Double Sleying—Putting two warp threads through each dent of reed.

Doups—Half-heddles for making loom-controlled gauze weaves.

Drafting—Plotting pattern on graph paper.

Drawing In—Threading the warp threads through reed and heddles.

Ends—Individual warp threads.

Fiber—The material, natural or synthetic, from which yarn is spun.

Filament—A long, continuous fiber, natural or synthetic.

Fly Shuttle—Shuttle thrown back and forth mechanically.

Gauze—Open weave made by twisting warp threads around each other. Also called leno.

Half-Sleying—Putting a warp thread through every other dent of a reed.

Harness—Frame to raise and lower warp threads. Also called shaft.

Haute Lisse—See High Warp.

Heading—Beginning and ending band of fabric.

Heddle—Wire or string with an eye through which the warp thread passes.

High Warp (Haute Lisse)—Warp running vertically on upright loom.

Lams—Parts of the floor loom to which harnesses are tied from above and treadles from below. Serve to balance harnesses and make possible multiple tie-ups. Also called marches.

Lease—See Cross.

Lease Rods—Sticks that keep alternating warp threads in order during warping and on loom. Also called cross rods.

Leno—See Gauze.

Lever—Mechanism that raises the harness on table looms. Same as treadle.

Lift—Process of raising one or more harnesses.

Low Warp (Basse Lisse)—Warp running horizontally from front to back of loom.

Macramé—Technique of knotting threads or strings.

Marches—See Lams.

Overshot—Weft threads that skip over groups of warp threads.

Pattern Weave—Design formed by threading and treadling arrangements.

Pedals—See Treadle.

Pick—One line of weft put through the warp. Also called a shot.

Pick-Up Stick—Flat stick for making hand-controlled patterns.

Pile—Yarns that make a surface raised above a flat background.

Plain Weave—Simple over-and-under interlocking of warp and weft.

Profile Draft—Short draft that indicates size of threading repeats.

Quill—See Bobbin.

Ratchet Wheels (Dogs)—Wheels on front and back rollers of loom with teeth into which a pawl or tongue falls. This permits motion of beam in one direction only.

Reed—Removable part of the beater which spreads the warp.

Rug Shuttle—Large shuttle for heavy yarn.

Selvage (Selvedge)—Side or edge of fabric.

Sett—The number of warp threads used per inch.

Shaft—See Harness.

Shed—opening in warp through which shuttle passes.

Shot—See Pick.

Shuttle—The device that carries the weft or filling yarn through the warp.

Shuttle Race—Protruding ledge in front of reed on beater.

Single Sleying—Putting one warp thread through each dent of the reed.

Skein Winder—Device for holding skeins of yarn for winding.

Sleying—Putting the warp threads through the dents of the reed.

Spooler—A bobbin winder.

Spool Rack—Rack for holding spools.

Stick Shuttle—Flat shuttle.

Sword—Flat stick used on primitive looms to separate the warp threads and press the weft into the warp.

Tabby—Plain weave. Also, the binding thread between pattern picks.

Template or Templet—Stretcher to prevent narrowing of cloth during weaving.

Tension—Tightness or looseness of warp threads.

Thread—In weaving terminology, a synonym for yarn.

Threading—Drawing warp threads through heddles and reed. Also called drawing in.

Threading Hook—Small hook used to draw warp threads through heddles and dents.

Thrums—Ends of warp left in reed and harnesses which cannot be woven.

Tie-up—(1) Linking of harnesses to lams and to treadles. (2) Combination of harnesses to form pattern.

Treadle—Mechanism to raise or lower harnesses.

Treadling—Sequence in which harness combinations are used.

Twill—Weave construction that is characterized by diagonal lines.

Twist—The direction in which a yarn is twisted in spinning or plying.

Warp—Threads stretched lengthwise on the loom.

Warp Beam—Roller in back of a loom on which the warp is wound.

Warp Chain—Warp threads counted and measured for winding on a loom.

Warping Board—A pegged rectangular or square board for making warps of short lengths.

Warp Sticks—Sticks laid between layers of warp on warp beam to keep their tension even.

Warp Tensioner—Device used to maintain sequence and tension of threads while warping a sectional warp beam.

Warp Tree or Reel—Device that turns on center spindle, used for making long chain warps.

Weaving—Interlacing of warp and weft threads to form a fabric.

Web—The part of a warp that is woven.

Weft—Threads crossing the width of the warp. Also called woof or filling.

Yardage Counter—Device that measures warp while it is being wound.

Yarn—A continuous thread spun from natural or synthetic fibers or filaments.

BIBLIOGRAPHY

FIBERS AND YARN

Baity, Elizabeth Chesley. *Man Is a Weaver.* New York: Viking, 1942.

Bendure, Zelma, and Pfeiffer, Gladys. *America's Fabrics.* New York: Macmillan, 1946.

Birrell, Verla. *The Textile Arts.* New York: Harper, 1959.

Blumenau, Lili. *The Art and Craft of Handweaving: Including Fabric Design.* New York: Crown, 1955.

Bolton, Eileen M. *Lichens for Vegetable Dyeing.* Newton Centre, Mass.: Branford.

Crawford, M. D. C., *The Heritage of Cotton.* New York: Putnam, 1948.

American Fabrics Encyclopedia of Textiles. New York: Doric, 1960.

Hollen, Norma, and Saddler, Jane. *Textiles.* 3d ed. New York: Macmillan, 1963.

Linton, George E. *Applied Textiles.* 4th ed. Metuchen, N. J.: Textile Book Service, 1948.

Matthews, J. Merritt. *The Textile Fibers.* 5th ed. London: Wiley, 1947.

Potter, David M. and Corbman, Bernard. *Textiles: Fiber to Fabric.* 4th ed. New York: Gregg, 1967.

Weibel, Adele Coulin. *Two Thousand Years of Textiles.* New York: Random House, 1952.

Wingate, I. B., ed. *Dictionary of Textiles.* 5th ed. New York: Fairchild, 1967.

COLOR AND DESIGN

Albers, Anni. *On Designing.* New Haven: Pellango Press, 1959.

Albers, Josef. *Interaction of Color.* New Haven: Yale University Press, 1963.

Bain, Robert. *The Clans and Tartans of Scotland.* London: Collins, 1947.

Blumenau, Lili. *Creative Design in Wallhanging.* New York: Crown, 1967.

Forman, B. and W., and Wassef, Ramses Wissa. *Tapestries from Egypt Woven by the Children or Harrania.* London: Hamlyn, 1961.

Graves, Maitland. *The Art of Color and Design.* New York: McGraw-Hill, 1941.

Hornung's Handbook of Designs and Devices. 2nd rev. ed. New York: Dover, 1946.

Innes of Learney, Sir Thomas. *The Tartans of the Clans and Families of Scotland.* 3rd ed. Edinburgh and London: M. and A. K. Johnston, 1948.

Johnston, Meda P., and Kaufman, Glen. *Design on Fabrics.* New York: Reinhold, 1967.

Kelley, Charles F., and Gentles, Margaret O. *Oriental Rugs.* Chicago: The Art Institute of Chicago, 1949.

Kybalova, Ludmila. *Contemporary Tapestries from Czechoslovakia.* London: Hamlyn, 1964.

———. *Coptic Textiles.* London: Hamlyn, 1967.

Laliberte, Norman, and Mogelon, Alex. *Banners and Hangings.* New York: Reinhold, 1966.

Maile, Anne. *Tie-and-Dye as a Present-Day Craft.* London: Mills and Boon, 1963.

Mason, J. Alden. *The Ancient Civilizations of Peru.* Rev. ed. Baltimore: Penguin Books, 1961.

Mayer, Christa C. *Masterpieces of Western Textiles from the Art Institute of Chicago.* Chicago: The Art Institute of Chicago, 1969.

The Metropolitan Museum of Art. *Handbook to the Loan Exhibition of French Tapestries—Medieval, Renaissance, and Modern.* New York: The Metropolitan Museum of Art, 1947.

O'Neale, Lila. *Textiles of Highland Guatemala.* Carnegie Institution of Washington Publication No. 567. Washington, D.C.: Carnegie Institution of Washington, 1945.

Osborne, Lilly de Jongh. *Indian Crafts of Guatemala and El Salvador.* Civilization of the American Indian Series, No. 2. Norman, Oklahoma: The University of Oklahoma Press, 1965.

Plath, Iona. *The Decorative Arts of Sweden.* New York: Dover, 1965.

Rodier, Paul. *The Romance of French Weaving.* New York: Tudor, 1936.

Rogers, Meyric R. *American Interior Design.* New York: Norton, 1947.

Ruskin, John. *The Art Criticism of John Ruskin.* Edited by R. L. Herbert. Garden City, New York: Doubleday, 1964.

Scheidig, Walker. *Crafts of the Bauhaus.* New York: Reinhold, 1967.

Sloane, Patricia. *Color: Basic Principles and New Directions.* New York: Reinhold, 1968.

Jobé, Joseph, ed. *Great Tapestries: The Web of History from the 12th to the 20th Century.* Translated by Peggy Rovell and Edita Lausanne Oberson. New York: Time-Life Books, 1965.

Yamanobe, Tomoyuki. *Textiles.* Arts and Crafts of Japan Series no. 2. English adaptation by Lynn Katoh. Rutland, Vermont: Tuttle, 1957.

WEAVING

Albers, Anni. *On Weaving.* Middleton, Conn.: Wesleyan University Press, 1965.

Allard, Mary. *Rug Making: Techniques and Design.* New York: Chilton, 1963.

Allen, Edith L. *Weaving You Can Do.* Peoria, Illinois: Manual Arts Press, 1947.

Allen, Helen L. *American and European Handweaving.* Rev. ed. Madison, Wisconsin: Democrat Weaving Co., 1939.

Amsden, Charles A. *Navajo Weaving: Its Technique and History.* Albuquerque: University of New Mexico Press, 1949.

Arnold, Ruth. *Weaving on a Drawloom.* 2 vols. Otis, Mass.: Arnold, 1956.

Atwater, Mary M. *The Shuttle-Craft Book of American Handweaving.* Rev. ed. New York: Macmillan, 1969.

———. *Byways in Hand-weaving.* Rev. ed. New York: Macmillan, 1967.

Beutlich, Tadek. *The Technique of Woven Tapestry.* New York: Watson-Guptill, 1967.

Birell, Verla. *The Textile Arts.* New York: Harper, 1959.

Black, Mary E. *New Key to Weaving.* Rev. ed. Milwaukee: Bruce, 1957.

Blum, Grace. *Functional Overshot.* Chicago: Grace Blum.

Blumenau, Lili. *The Art and Craft of Handweaving.* New York: Crown, 1968.

———. *Creative Design in Wallhangings.* New York: Crown, 1967.

Brown, Harriett J. *Handweaving for Pleasure and Profit.* New York: Harper, 1952.

Collingwood, Peter. *The Techniques of Rug Weaving.* New York: Watson-Guptill, 1969.

Conrad, Elvira. "Back-Strap Looms Used by Weavers in Hawaii." *Handweaver and Craftsman,* Vol. 14, No. 3 (1963).

Cyrus, Ulla. *Manual of Swedish Handweaving.* Translated by Viola Anderson. Newton Centre, Mass.: Branford, 1956.

Davison, Marguerite Porter. *A Handweaver's Pattern Book.* Rev. ed. Swarthmore, Pa.: Marguerite P. Davison, 1951.

D'Harcourt, Raoul, et. al., eds. *Textiles of Ancient Peru and Their Techniques.* Translated by Sadie Brown. Seattle: The University of Washington Press, 1962.

Emery, Irene. *Primary Structures of Fabrics.* Washington, D.C.: Textile Museum, 1966.

Frey, Berta. *Designing and Drafting for Handweavers.* New York: Macmillan, 1958.

Gräbner, Ernst. *Die Weberei.* Leipzig: Fachbuchverlag, 1951.

Greer, Gertrude. *Adventures in Weaving.* Peoria, Illinois: Manual Arts Press, 1951.

Grierson, Ronald. *Woven Rugs.* 2nd ed. Leicester, England: Dryad, 1960.

Harvey, Virginia I. *Macramé: The Art of Creative Knotting.* New York: Reinhold, 1966.

Hauptman, Bruno. *Gewebetechnik.* Leipzig: Fachbuchverlag, 1952.

Hooper, Luther. *Handloom Weaving, Plain and Ornamental.* Bath, England: Pitman, 1936.

Jacobsen, Charles W. *Oriental Rugs, A Complete Guide.* Rutland, Vermont: Tuttle, 1962.

Kaufmann, Ruth. *New American Tapestry.* New York: Reinhold, 1968.

Kirby, Mary. *Designing on the Loom.* London: Studio, 1955.

Maxwell, Gilbert S. and Conrotto, E. L., *Navajo Rugs.* Palm Desert, Calif.: Desert-Southwest, Inc.

Millen, Rogers. *Weave Your Own Tweeds.* Swarthmore, Pa.: Marguerite P. Davison, 1948.

Moseley, Johnson and Koenig. *Craft Design.* Belmont, Calif.: Wadsworth, 1962.

Oelsner, G. H., and Dale, Samuel. *Handbook of Weaves.* New York: Dover, 1951.

Overman, Ruth, and Smith, Lula. *Contemporary Handweaving.* Ames, Iowa: Iowa State University Press, 1955.

Pyysalo, Helvi, and Merisalo, Viivi, *Handweaving Patterns from Finland.* Translated by Bertha B. Needham and Aili J. Marsh. Newton Centre, Mass.: Branford, 1960.

Rainey, Sarita R. *Weaving Without a Loom.* Worcester, Mass.: Davis, 1966.

Rinde-Ramsback, Marta, and Lundback, Maja. *Small Webs.* Translated by Gerda M. Anderson. Stockholm: ICA-Förlaget, 1936.

Roth H. Ling. *Studies in Primitive Looms.* 3rd ed. Halifax, England: Bankfield Museum, 1950.

Salet, F. *La Tapisserie Française du Moyen Age à Nos Jours.* Paris: Vincent Féreal, 1946.

Selander, Malin. *Swedish Hand Weaving: Weaving Patterns.* Translated by Alice Griswold and Karin Haskonsen. Göteborg: Wezata Förlag, 1956.

Simpson, L. E., and Weir, N. *The Weaver's Craft.* 6th rev. ed. Peoria, Illinois: Manual Arts Press, 1946.

Tattersall, C. E. C. *Notes on Carpet Knotting and Weaving.* London: Victoria and Albert Museum, 1961.

Thorpe, Azalea, and Larson, Jack L. *Elements of Weaving.* Edited by Mary Lyon. Garden City, New York: Doubleday, 1967.

Tidball, Harriet. *The Weaver's Book.* New York: Macmillan, 1961.

Tod, Osma. *The Joy of Handweaving.* Princeton: D. Van Nostrand, 1964.

Tovey, John. *The Technique of Weaving.* New York: Reinhold, 1966.

BIBLIOGRAPHY (Continued)

Trotzig, Livack, and Axelson, A. *Band.* Stockholm: ICA-Förlaget.

Watson, William. *Textile Design and Color.* London: Longmans.

——.*Advanced Textile Design.* London: Longmans, 1946.

West, Virginia. *Finishing Touches for the Handweaver.* Newton Centre, Mass.: Branford, 1967.

Wilson, Jean. *Weaving Is for Anyone.* New York: Reinhold, 1966.

Worst, Edward F. *Footpower Loom Weaving.* Milwaukee: Bruce.

——.*How to Weave Linens.* Milwaukee: Bruce, 1948.

Zielinski, S. A. *Encyclopedia of Hand Weaving.* New York: Funk and Wagnalls, 1959.

Znamierowski, Nell. *Step by Step Weaving.* New York: Golden Press, 1967.

THE SHUTTLE CRAFT GUILD PUBLICATIONS (SHUTTLECRAFT GUILD MONOGRAPHS)

Atwater, Mary M. *Guatemala Visited.*

Harvey, Virginia I., and Tidball, Harriet. *Weft Twining.*

Rhodes, T. S. *Color Related Decorating Textiles.*

Tidball, Harriet. *Brocade.*

——. *Contemporary Satins.*

——. *Contemporary Tapestry.*

——. *Double Weave.*

——. *Handloom Weaves.*

——. *Handwoven Specialties.*

——. *Inkle Weave.*

——. *Mexican Motifs.*

——. *Peru: Textiles Unlimited.* Parts I and II.

——. *Summer and Winter Weave.*

——. *Supplemental Warp Patterning.*

——. *Surface Interest: Textiles of Today.*

——. *Textile Structure: Drafts and Analysis.*

——. *Two-Harness Textiles: The Loom-Controlled Weaves.*

——. *Two-Harness Textiles: The Open-Work Weaves.*

——. *Undulating Weft Effects.*

——. *Weaver's Book of Scottish Tartans.*

Note: All Shuttlecraft monographs are distributed by the Craft and Hobby Book Service, P.O. Box 626, Pacific Grove, California, 93950, and by the Shuttle Craft Guild, 4499 Delta River Drive, Lansing, Mich., 48906.

PERIODICALS ON WEAVING

American Fabrics (Quarterly)
Doric Publishing Company
24 E. 38th Street
New York, New York 10016

Bulletin of Ontario Handweavers and Spinners
1166 Adelaide Street N.
London, Ontario, Canada

Craft Horizons (Quarterly)
American Craftsmen's Council
44 West 53rd Street
New York, New York 10019

du Pont Magazine (Bi-monthly)
E. I. du Pont de Nemours & Company
Wilmington, Delaware

Handweaver and Craftsman
220 Fifth Avenue
New York, New York 10001

Index to Handweaver and Craftsman Magazine
Judith Arness
3915 Washington Street
Kensington, Maryland 20795

The Master Weaver
A-Handicrafts
Fulford, P.Q., Canada

Quarterly Journal of the Guilds of Weavers, Spinners and Dyers
1 Harrington Road
Brighton 6, England

Shuttle, Spindle & Dye-pot (Members of Handweavers Guild of America only)
339 N. Steele Road
West Hartford, Conn. 06117

Warp and Weft
Robin & Russ
533 N. Adams St.
McMinnville, Ore. 97128

SUPPLIERS SPECIALIZING IN WEAVING BOOKS AND MAGAZINES

Craft and Hobby Book Service
P.O. Box 626
Pacific Grove, California 93950

K. R. Drummond, Bookseller
Hart Grove
Ealing Common
London W.5, England

Museum Books, Incorporated
48 E. 43rd Street
New York, New York 10017

The Unicorn Books for Craftsmen
P.O. Box 645
Rockville, Maryland 20851

SUPPLIERS OF BOOKLETS TO THE TRADE

Celanese Corporation of America
180 Madison Avenue
New York, New York

National Cotton Council of America
P.O. Box 12285
Memphis, Tennessee

S. Stroock & Co., Inc.
404 5th Avenue
New York, New York

The Wool Bureau, Inc.
16 W. 46th Street
New York, New York 10036

Desert-Southwest, Inc.
P.O. Box 757
Palm Desert, California

Textile Book Service
521 Liberty
Metuchen, New Jersey

INDEX